the English room

For Gene with much
love for being a
wonderful Nanny!

Chippy Irvine

October 25th 2003

the English room

Chippy Irvine

introduction by Keith Irvine
photographs by Christopher Simon Sykes

A BULFINCH PRESS BOOK
LITTLE, BROWN AND COMPANY
BOSTON NEW YORK LONDON

THIS BOOK IS DEDICATED BY CHIPPY AND KEITH IRVINE TO THE MEMORY

OF THEIR MENTORS,

MADGE GARLAND AND JOHN FOWLER.

ISBN 0-8212-2705-X
Library of Congress Control Number 2001090606

First published in Great Britain in 2001 by
Pavilion Books Limited

Designed by David Fordham

Bulfinch Press is an imprint and trademark of Little, Brown and Company (Inc.).

Printed in Italy

Page 1
Painter Richard Beer's sitting room in Regent's Park, London. The bronze plaster bust was originally used for display in an 1890s French shop.
Page 2
An interior mews courtyard designed in the early 18th century by architect William Kent.
Page 6
The Jacobean staircase at Eyam Hall in the Peak District of Derbyshire, which dates from 1671.

ACKNOWLEDGMENTS

I'd like to thank Christopher Simon Sykes, not only for his *puissant* and stylish photographs, but also for his companionship and brilliant navigation of England's towns
and countryside as we photographed a variety of English rooms. He once remarked, "If you travel with me, you will never go hungry," and I found this to be true.
There are others to be thanked: for giving information, contacts, for offering hospitality from cups of tea to sumptuous meals and overnight accommodation, for unlocking
doors, and generally being wonderfully helpful. Among the many are Justin Meath Baker, Robin and Jacqueline Basker, Doris Bieber, Elisabeth Bowden, Monkey
Chambers, Sybilla Clark, Adrian Csarky, Mark and Val Elwes, Jean Goddard, Brian Godbold, Jenny Gray, Kitty Grime, Anissa Helou, David Hogg, Michael and Anne
Johnston, Shirley Kelly, Joyce Khedoory, Dede Lassoe, Stephen Long, Min Hogg, Philip Mehew and Angela Truelove, Lady Jean Nevile, Christopher Nevile, Susan
Palmer, Anna Price, David and Shervie Price, Dede Regan, John Reed, Imogen Taylor, David Sassoon, Raffaela Barker St Clair, Guy Taplin, Mariann Wasser, plus
many more who probably for good reasons prefer to remain anonymous.
I'd like to thank my English publisher, Pavilion, who originally approached my husband, Keith, to write this book. Because he has such a busy life as a New York interior
decorator, this was impossible, but Colin Webb and Vivien James at Pavilion were able to negotiate with my long-time agent, Angela Miller, and they let me have a go
instead. I worked with editors Morwenna Wallis, Kate Oldfield and Anthea Snow, all of whom were patient and endlessly helpful, even when bullying me to dig out ever
more obscure details. David Fordham designed the book to make all the photographs enhance one another. As I look at them now, I have happy memories of the good
times and the generous people who helped to make it possible.

contents:

town

country

foreword

HAVING BEEN A PROFESSIONAL INTERIOR DECORATOR for 45 years and spent half my life in Britain and half in the United States, houses and the rooms in them have been a constant interest. As the youngest of three children and the last to live at home in Nairn, Scotland, I accompanied my peripatetic father on endless excursions to famous castles and stately – and sub-stately – homes, often long before they were open to the general public. My father was a keen history buff, and a wanderer. We would motor far afield, especially if that day's target was close to a good golf course or known trout stream. He was interested in the family history of each place we visited and I became subliminally fascinated by the gardens, architecture, and dispositions of rooms and furniture.

Though continuing to be an observer and an omnivorous reader about architecture and the decorative arts, this had no direct influence on my career until I was in my twenties. After a sojourn at the newly opened Interior Design School, established by Sir Hugh Casson as professor at the Royal College of Art (where Chippy and I first met), I landed a job as assistant to the now-legendary John Fowler. I found him to be an irascible, knowledgeable old man who overworked and underpaid me. It was an invaluable learning experience as my eyes were opened and my ideas expanded by this *éminence grise* of our profession. In the 1950s Colefax & Fowler was bought by that redoubtable American dilettante Nancy Lancaster. As a ghost-boss, Mrs. Lancaster brought an injection of high-style transatlantic flair that enhanced Mr. Fowler's erudite and studious knowledge. The cash registers started ringing and soon the so-called "English Country House look" was up and running. This was a creative interpretation in the mid-20th century of a quality to which English rooms had aspired for many centuries. Its effect, adapted and "watered down" is still a strong influence in English houses today. The magazines dealing with interior design have transmuted it as a staple of ideas for masses of people, who can apply it to their modes of living by using Fowler's credo of "comfort and suitability" and edge of "pleasing decay." This latter quality suits (and always has) the British character, which is literary, trenchant, and undemonstrative, but full of confidence. Most English rooms fit comfortably, like an old shoe. The subtle charm and idiosyncrasies of English rooms have been excellently caught in Christopher Simon Sykes's stylish and evocative photographs, most of which have been specially commissioned for this book.

The English Room deftly encapsulates the development of English architectural history and modes of life over the past few centuries – both in urban settings and in the unmatched English countryside – indicating how our past illuminates where we may be going. In this new century we will surely take many exciting, and, as yet, unpredictable steps forward. Whatever global influences, new technologies, and advances in interior design may evolve, certain styles will inevitably be reinvented, absorbed, and adapted – as they always have been by the English – creating spaces for living with resilient flair and spirit.

KEITH B. IRVINE

town

introduction

The English character, like the English language, is formed from a mélange of cultural influences, stretching back to the time of the Anglo-Saxons and forward to a continuing influx of new citizens. The country's architecture and interiors – its houses and their individual rooms – have been affected by geography, climate, politics, and technology, but most of all by the flair of its inhabitants.

Although the English gentry have always been passionate about the countryside, since the Tudor period (1485–1558) it has also been important for them to have a house in town to attend to business and governmental affairs and to cut a dash among the influential elite.

Architect Inigo Jones (1573–1652) was primarily responsible for moving England's buildings away from the medieval style with its gables, turrets, and bay windows and into the new Palladian Classicism. Startlingly chaste, this Classical style was not to become fashionable in England for almost another century, when it blossomed as the Georgian style. Jones also introduced an innovation in town planning, the square. The first of these was built in London's Covent Garden on the Duke of Bedford's estate, and the idea was later taken up by developers in the 18th century to enhance the appearance of many English towns, as well as influencing the planning of American cities such as Savannah and Philadelphia.

London has undergone more transformations than any English town or city, sometimes dramatic ones, as in 1666 when the Great Fire roared through its tightly packed medieval wooden buildings, destroying two thirds of the city. Disaster though it was, the fire cleansed London of the Great Plague and made way for the building of churches in the Classical Baroque style under Sir Christopher Wren (1632–1723). It also allowed for expansion, as newly wealthy families built in the area known as the West End.

The boroughs of London expanded between 1660 and 1745. Dwellings took the form of simple brick row houses or free-standing houses. Where the Baroque of Wren, Nicholas Hawksmoor (1661–1736), and Sir John Vanbrugh (1664–1726) appealed to the elite and owed inspiration to the grandeur of Rome and Paris, less pretentious borough houses and their gardens were more akin to those in Holland, where the spice trade with the East Indies had enabled the growth of a prosperous middle class, who lavished attention on the quality and domesticity of their interiors while avoiding any fussiness or pomp. Technical advances followed, such as larger panes of glass, sash windows, efficient chimneys and smaller fireplaces, which added comfort.

During the first part of the 17th century, there were also important breakthroughs in interior furnishings. Convertible furniture developed, such as settles that had seats which opened to give storage room and backs that swung over to form a table. Ubiquitous chests were finally stacked up to form a single "chest of drawers." "Falling tables" were invented, with tilt-up tops. The stick-back or Windsor chair appeared in the houses of the yeomanry, and seat furniture began to acquire permanent upholstery.

By the 18th century, England was enjoying a relatively long period of domestic peace, and with it more prosperity. A return to the proportion and discipline of Classical architecture, in the early flowering of Georgian architecture, was introduced by important figures such as Colen Campbell (1676–1729), Lord Burlington (1694–1753), and William Kent (1685–1748). Kent studied painting in Rome for 10 years and can be considered England's first "internal" decorator. By 1715 he had designed a garden in an informal park-like style anticipating the renowned garden designer Lancelot (Capability) Brown (1716–83), and he went on to design houses, interiors, furniture, and painted decorations. As other architects took up the Classical style, cities all over England developed streets and crescents of Georgian elegance, the ancient spa town of Bath being one of the best-preserved examples.

The 18th century also saw the growth of the furniture-making industry, centered around three skilled and inspired tradesmen: Thomas Chippendale (1718–79), George Hepplewhite (died 1786) and Thomas Sheraton (1751–1806). Busy workshops supplied a growing number of cultivated patrons. For the wealthy, a full education included the Grand Tour – a journey round Europe, and especially Italy, that could last from a few months to several years, during which vast numbers of paintings, sculptures, folios, and curiosities were shipped back to England. Such collections had previously been assembled by royalty or the extremely rich and often displayed in private rooms copied from the French and Dutch and known as "cabinets." Now the acquirement of Taste was seen as a badge of personal civilization by a much larger but still elite group, and a great deal of attention was given to the display of collections, adding an intellectual edge to rooms and inspiring their decoration. Walls were covered with paintings other than ancestral portraits, such as landscapes, still lifes, and nudes. Niches for statues punctuated grand rooms, corridors, and staircases. Libraries were stocked with illustrated volumes of botanicals. Lacquered cabinets were imported or created by skilled cabinet-makers in order to hold collections of biological specimens or bibelots.

In the late 18th century, a new, lighter style of interior decoration became fashionable, to replace the vigorous Kentian grotesques. This neo-Classical mode was inspired by archeological investigations at ancient sites such as Pompeii and Herculaneum, which uncovered miraculously preserved mosaics, wall paintings, and artifacts. The neo-Classical style was elevated to an art by Robert Adam (1728–92) who, like Kent, combined architecture and interior decoration to produce an integrated design. Adam also spent time in Italy, and on his return developed his own completely idiosyncratic style that drew on a wide range of Classical motifs and archeological knowledge, including the so-called Etruscan style, a more delicate look than the power-hungry style of Rome that was in fact related to Greek colonies in Italy. He decorated walls and ceilings in finely worked plaster picked out in pretty colors, and often a ceiling decoration would be mirrored in the pattern of the carpet below.

With greater access to Greece in the late 18th century, this ancient civilization and its architecture and artifacts caught the imagination, creating a passion that lasted into the Regency period. An increase in travel, and archeological discoveries informed by more accurate scholarship, added Palmyra, Baalbek, Spalato, and Egypt as sources for an already wide mix of design motifs. Regency interior design, as well as clothes, manners and taste, translated and combined many themes into a self-conscious eclecticism, seen at its over-the-top height at the Royal Pavilion (between 1784 and 1827) at Brighton, which combines Indian and Chinoiserie styles.

It was not until the beginning of the 19th century that beaches became fashionable as summer resorts, and the benefits of sea air began to be promoted. Brighton developed around the Royal Pavilion, and other resorts spread along the south coast. Many of the seaside houses were called "villas" and were built in a light-hearted Regency style, ornamented with lacily carved bargeboards that hint at "Gothick" fantasies or decorated whimsically in a cottage *orné* style. During this period, there was an increased use of window bays and of interiors that led outdoors via French or "Italian" windows. It also became fashionable to have rooms leading from one to another in an open plan, divided by arches or columns, or with optional folding doors. These developed into the sliding doors popular in the mid-Victorian period.

In the early 19th century, one of London's most influential transformers was not an architect but the enterprising builder and developer Thomas Cubitt (1788–1855), who was responsible for many of the elegant terrace houses that line the city's streets. Terrace houses were not new – John Nash had designed magnificent neo-Classical examples in Regent's Park – but the major part of Cubitt's building, in the 1830s and 1840s, was intended for slightly less wealthy families, though they are much sought-after now. Based on neo-Classical principles and built with an attention to pleasing visual proportions, they recast the look of London. A feature of these houses was their arrangement in a block with the front doors facing a generously wide street and the backs facing a shared green space for walking or in which children could play. The greenery played well against the uniformity of the cream-painted stucco houses. Other developers followed suit, so that London is now blessed with whole neighborhoods of handsome terrace houses in tree-lined streets.

One of the most idiosyncratic town houses of the early 19th century is that of architect Sir John Soane at Lincoln's Inn in London. Soane's ingenious use of natural light sources, often concealed from view, his clever way of cramming antique architectural fragments into pleasing arrangements, and his space-saving invention for the display of pictures using three layers of boards that swing out on hinges and can be fitted back into the walls, were all ahead of their time and yet clearly English in their intellectual eccentricity.

In the 1820s, there was a short period when the decorative arts and fashion paused on the brink of the Victorian age. The British colonies were growing and England was the center of commerce. Napoleon had earlier declared that England was a nation of shopkeepers, but it was now a nation of luxury goods retailers. This was the era of *Le Style Melbourne* (William Lamb Melbourne was Queen Victoria's first Prime Minister) and of the Whig men's clubs. Furnishings took on their most masculine turn since the beginning of the 18th century, and inventive mechanical furniture, such as wheelchairs and book rests on armchairs, began to be manufactured. Made mostly of mahogany, this furniture was solid, heavy, and untrimmed.

The Victorian period saw interiors gradually becoming cluttered with a series of pseudo-historical architectural revivals, including Gothic – now rather preachy and pious – Italianate, Elizabethan, and Louis XVI, each following on the other's heels and by the 1880s mixed up together with exuberant license. Furniture and fabric was now manufactured comparatively inexpensively and vast amounts were bought by the growing population. The Great Exhibition of 1851 encouraged manufacturing, and this was joined by a temptation to over-embellish. Swags of cloth draped windows, while portières hung on brass or wooden rings rattled on drawing-room doors. Tufted sofas and armchairs, heavy with bullion fringe, formed an obstacle course across violently colored Kidderminster and Axminster carpets. Knick-knacks and holiday souvenirs were crammed onto whatnots. Candlesticks, whose use had been supplanted by the oil-fueled argand lamp or by gas lamps, were lined up with clocks and figurines on the mantelpiece, from which hung crimson fringed plush. No surface was left plain – it was a great time for doilies and antimacassars.

William Morris (1834–96), poet, designer, and champion of the working man, deplored the effect that industrial mechanization was having in England and instigated the Arts and Crafts Movement, which revived traditional handicrafts and building techniques. He fostered a distinctive look in fabric, wallpaper, and furniture as well as in stained glass and embroidery, partly inspired by medieval designs. The wallpapers, some by illustrator Walter Crane, included an overall design and a dado to define the height of what traditionally had been a chair rail, plus a border or frieze to give a crown edging to a room. Furniture, at least to begin with, was hand made. Some pieces included elaborate inlaid work, but the characteristic items were simple – what came to be called "cottage furniture." Though intended to present "artistic" interior design for the general public, the advances made by industrialization and the availability of inexpensive goods meant that only the well-to-do could afford these products. The movement prevailed in various forms into the 1920s, producing houses with leaded panes, window seats, low ceilings, artistically tiled fireplaces, and practical kitchens.

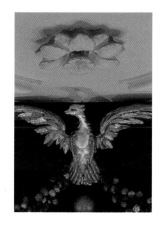

Victorian revivalism led to an eclectic use of Tudor half-timbering, "Queen Anne" style, and other vernacular forms. These buildings bore little resemblance to their namesakes, but their asymmetrical design and fanciful details, such as turrets at the corners, gave a small-scale romance to the growing suburbs. One of the most influential architects during this period was Norman Shaw (1831–1912), whose clients, the well-to-do upper-middle class, wanted to live in detached houses rather than terraces. Many of his houses still exist in Chelsea and especially in Chiswick, an area being developed around 1900. This was the beginning of a distinct Edwardian look. Within 20 years of his heyday, developers had taken up the style and built smaller, less expensive houses in the same vein in towns all over England. These were usually no more than three stories high with small front gardens but often larger gardens, sometimes with an allotment, at the back. The interiors were treated to a lot of dark wood highlighted with white paint. They included twisting staircases and inglenooks, bow and casement windows with lead panes, artistic tiles, and upholstery of cozy cretonne.

Art Nouveau was a short-lived but influential style that lasted from around 1890 to 1901. As the name indicates it was a French style, a somewhat foreign incursion onto the usually less frivolous English taste. It incorporated two distinct artistic veins. One was composed of sinuous vines based loosely on natural forms, while the other was more austere, with vertical rectilinear interiors and furniture invented by the Glasgow School designer Charles Rennie Mackintosh (1868–1928). It was the latter style that led to the Modern Movement, ushered into England by a house designed by Erich Mendelsohn (1887–1953) in Old

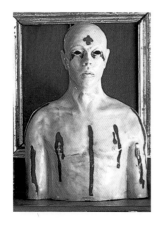

Church Street, Chelsea. This London street is worth studying as it includes many exemplary houses illustrating Georgian, Regency, Norman Shaw, Modern Movement, and International Style architecture.

Up until the First World War, town house interiors had a separate life above and below stairs, and a different style of decoration was adopted from floor to floor. Reception rooms used for formal entertainments were lavish, but bedrooms, bathrooms, and nurseries less so. The servants' quarters, below stairs and in attic bedrooms, were at best practical but plain. This lifestyle dwindled after the First World War. Owing to the exorbitant cost of real estate, many town houses in Central London have now been converted into apartments. The original use of their rooms has been altered to accommodate present-day needs, and bathrooms and mini kitchens have been added to each unit. London's early 19th-century terrace houses – the Cubitt building legacy – lend themselves to all kinds of modern conversions and interior decoration. These well-built terrace houses have large, well-proportioned windows, parquet floors, and – if they have not been ruthlessly stripped away – crown moldings and paneled doors.

Mews dwelling did not become desirable until after the First World War, when chic people were trying to make city life bearable minus servants. Originally, mews were small service streets tucked behind wider streets with grand houses. The ground floor of a mews cottage was a stable and carriage house, and the grooms lived above. From the late 1920s on, mews cottages reached a high level of smartness within a limited space, whether decorated with sofas and cushions influenced by the Russian Ballet, with crisp Vogue Regency stripes, or with antiques and pretty chintzes.

English domestic interiors for the wealthy city dweller in the 1920s and 1930s were shaped by the newly named profession of "interior decorating." Following in the footsteps of "the first lady decorator," as American Elsie de Wolfe (1865–1950) frequently described herself, Syrie Maugham, the wife of writer Somerset Maugham, opened her London shop in 1922. Maugham straddled Moderne and traditional styles and was famous for her modish "all-white" rooms (that were really more beige and off-white, and by no means her only color scheme) with mirrored walls that imparted an atmosphere of effortless luxe. She gained notoriety for stripping and "pickling" good 18th-century furniture to lighten the color. Sibyl Colefax started her business in London in 1934, specializing in Vogue Regency schemes, and was joined by John Fowler in 1938. Through diligent scholarship Fowler went on to become a restoration specialist and the most important English interior decorator of the 20th century. He provided an enlightened sense of style, luxury, and taste, imbuing each room with a sense that it had evolved over time.

The Moderne style developed from the Art Deco movement, which got its name in Paris at the Exposition Internationale des Arts Décoratifs et Industriels in 1925. A major theme was mirrors, accompanied by low sofas, black satin poofs, huge ashtrays, anything chrome or covered in shagreen or gold-flecked lacquer, a zebra-skin rug, and perhaps a single lily in a vase. The English found it cosmopolitan and madly smart. It lived on in the slightly racy, pared-down luxury of Thirties Retro.

Compared to the rambling sprawl of country houses, town architecture has a much more vertical thrust. However, the English did not take to self-contained, purpose-built apartments until the Edwardian era.

In London, a style informally known as "Pont Street Dutch" – named after the street where buildings were given pseudo Dutch façades – swept through the edges of Belgravia, Knightsbridge, and Kensington, catering to the new flat dweller. In the 1920s and 1930s blocks of less elaborately decorated buildings designed as luxury apartments sprang up in Mayfair and other affluent areas, while the building of efficiency flats began in less prosperous districts. Watered-down versions of the International Style gave a modern look to apartment blocks, which was reflected in their interiors.

Rooming houses existed in English towns since around the 16th century. The bedsitter was a mid-20th-century version of this, ideal for students and low-income workers. A gas ring in a corner was provided for cooking, and a shared bathroom was down the hall, where four pennies fed into a meter would supply enough warm water for a bath. The style of decor was usually the landlord's cast-offs, and ingenuity and imagination were needed to make these homes look attractive. Ceilings draped with Indian bedspreads, floor cushions covered with African kente cloth, Japanese tatami mats, and increasingly available museum posters, created temporary, stylish quarters for the less well-off after the Second World War.

Interior design was regarded with ambivalence in post-War England, though its towns were starved of stylish elegance. The English often have strong feelings about taste and quality, believing that it indicates "good breeding," but are fearful of being too smart and slick. Many were, and still are, averse to employing an interior decorator. Traditionally trained decorators went on providing beautiful, almost dateless rooms for a privileged few after the Second World War, but class distinctions, once so powerful in England, were beginning to break down. Decorator David Hicks was able to pull these forces together into a fresh cosmopolitan style of interior design. He took American ideas and Europeanized them, combining novelties such as Lucite tables, side tables made from mirrored glass cubes, and dark-brown satin sofas, and anchoring them on his distinctive carpets, patterned in tiny geometrics.

The Preservation Movement of the 1970s affected city life as well as country houses. After two decades of pulling down obsolete industrial buildings, warehouses acquired fashionable appeal and were renovated into desirable, spacious lofts for modern urbanites. Style at the turn of the 21st century for these city dwellers tended toward neutral colors, geometric patterns – if any patterns were allowed – steel shelves, concrete walls, wood floors, leather and canvas upholstery, designer furniture, and mid-century retro. Carried to such extremes, minimalism had to swing back to a more colorful and romantic mien. Stripped-down interiors look wonderful until there is one smudge on the polished glass surface, or one scuff on the blond-wood floor. In spite of the fashion cry of "simplify, simplify," many people have found that these supposedly functional spaces require high maintenance.

For the truly English personality, rooms incorporate quirky touches, a mingling of experiences, something old and literate contrasting with something new and spirited, plenty of books, pictures, odd personal collections that have taken a lifetime or several to acquire, plus a wealth of forgiveness for worn patinas and threadbare fabric, providing it has intrinsic beauty. These qualities reflect the slightly – but not dangerously – eccentric English taste.

chapter 1

front rooms

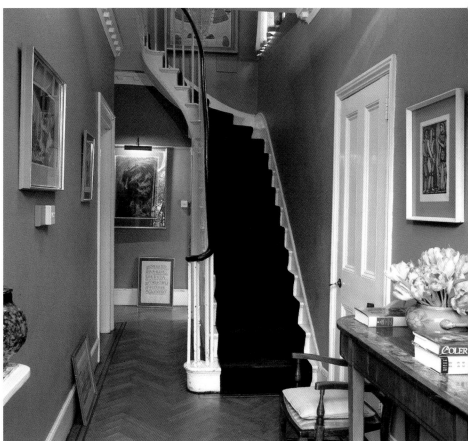

entrance *halls*,
drawing *rooms*, dining *rooms*
& living *rooms*

LEFT: Interior designer David Hare's drawing room has shuttered sash windows typical of 18th- and 19th-century London town houses built for the middle classes. Paint finishes are one of Hare's specialties and he has given this room subtle brown, dragged and painted walls and furnished it with a blend of his favorite antique Afghanistan and Uzbekistan textiles and Sousani embroideries.

ABOVE: The hallway of the house where the late poet Stephen Spender lived shows a traditional arrangement of polished parquet floor, strong colors and an eclectic mix of paintings.

ENTRANCE HALLS

THE APPROACH TO A HOUSE creates the first impression. The restrictions placed on space in towns and cities make long and imposing private drives impossible but, for the great town houses of the 17th and 18th century, courtyards created a splendid effect. Nothing is more impressive than the courtyard at Burlington House in London (remodelled 1718–19), once a private house but now the exhibition rooms for the Royal Academy of Art. The smaller 18th-century courtyard shown on page 2 was designed by William Kent in a London mews. Now, instead of ringing with the clatter of horses' hooves, the courtyard has become a place for alfresco relaxation in the heart of London. The passage shown opposite is within the stable buildings that lead off this courtyard, in one of a pair of mews houses combined by decorator John Fowler of Colefax & Fowler for clients in the 1950s. The conversion created an interesting, rambling space centered around the handsome inner courtyard with its huge arched doors.

More commonly, in the middle-class town houses of the 19th and early 20th century, clipped hedges or iron railings surrounded a small front garden. Steps usually led up to the front door, and for the upper middle classes this was often flanked by dignified pillars, a nod to the neo-Classical style of many of the grander London terrace houses. The door itself had a brass knocker, letter slot, and elegant numbers, polished every day by a maid. Steps also led down to the modest basement, clearly indicating that this was the servants' and tradespersons' entrance. Those servants who did not live in the same house as their employer, occupied small row houses whose doors opened right onto the street. The sign of a good housewife in such houses was a scrubbed front doorstep, which might be edged with white lime paste.

In middle-class houses, the front door was protected by a porch. The small, outer space provided a shelter while you unlocked the door. Inside, an anteroom had a second door that acted as a draft protector. In this area, there was space for a doormat and an umbrella stand, which were essential furnishings, and possibly also a coat stand with a hat rack and a looking glass.

The hallway beyond, in all but the wealthiest town houses, consisted of a passage with a staircase leading off it, such as the one shown on page 17 in the home of the late poet Sir Stephen Spender. Halls in many town houses ran straight through the length of the house and opened onto a garden at the back, as in the Clapham hallway shown on the left. This house belongs to garden designer Christopher Masson, who has made his continually changing back garden into the focus of the house. Furnishings in narrow halls such as these have to be sparse: a chair or bench to change shoes, an oak chest to hide away oddments, a grandfather clock, a hall stand or a table. The style of these furnishings has altered since the 19th century, but the need for them has remained consistent. One significant change has occurred, however, since the Second World War. Prior to this, in households that could afford servants, the hall incorporated a door covered in green baize (a felt-like fabric), which divided the owner's family from the kitchen and cleaning staff. In very small houses, those that were built for working-class families but which are now considered highly desirable, the hall is simply a narrow passage with room only for a bicycle or a row of coat hooks.

By contrast, aristocratic houses of the 18th and 19th century had large, rectangular halls with chairs placed against the walls. These hall chairs were deliberately designed to be uncomfortable, to discourage

ABOVE: This hall passage in the 1860 south London terrace house belonging to garden designer Christopher Masson draws the eye in all the way to the focal point of the house — the garden beyond.

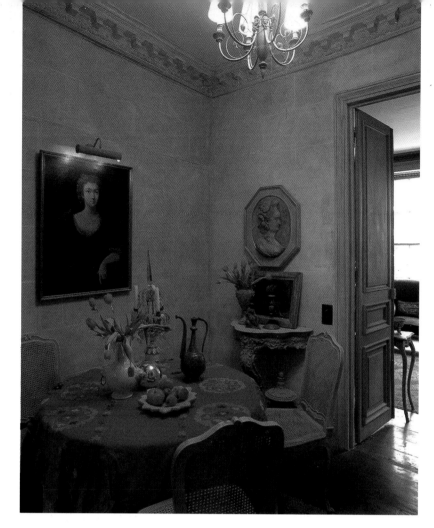

LEFT: Iranian interior designer Alidad Mahloudji used English elements, and yet produced a mysteriously exotic atmosphere, in the hall of his staid Mayfair apartment by padding the walls with donkey brown wool, then attaching medallions of historic characters cut from a printed furnishing fabric. The portraits were mounted on ovals edged with thick, brown cord knotted at the apex. The medallion motif is a nod to the late 17th- and early 18th-century portraits by Sir Godfrey Kneller and also echoes Alidad's collection of small antique oval plaster medallions. A head of Augustus presides on the hall table.

lesser mortals or petitioners from sitting for too long. The porter's chair, found in especially grand houses, was a bulky structure always kept near the front door. It was tufted, with the padding held in place by buttons, covered in sturdy leather, and had an enveloping hood to protect the porter on duty from drafts.

Occasionally, halls today are large enough to have a central table to hold flowers, large folio-style books, *objets de vertu*, and small collections reflecting the owner's taste, or have a statue in pride of place. The lobby in an apartment block, however, is impersonal and bland to a degree, in an attempt to offend no-one. It is not until one enters the private domain that the character of the owner begins to show. Designer Alidad Mahloudji has created a mysterious mood in his fabric-lined hall (left). As a collector of small antique portrait medallions, he has mimicked these by cutting oval-shaped motifs from fabric.

Interior designer David Hare's hall (above), though a tiny space, is used as an intimate dining area. Separate dining rooms are one of the casualties of the 20th-century conversion of houses into flats, and great ingenuity must be used when entertaining. Hare's dining room includes faux finishes, such as a wall painted to resemble blocks of stone. For those who lack skilled specialty painters to do this work, wallpapers are available that provide the effect of stone, ashlar, brick, or marble. The inspiration behind Hare's walls can be traced back to the impeccable masonry of the great 18th-century houses inspired by Palladio. Wallpaper that imitates fabric, or which has bold stripes with a contrasting border, has been used since the Regency period (1812–20). The striped wallpaper was revived in soft colours in the neo-Regency style of 1912–20 and, using snappier colours, in the 1940s and 1950s as Vogue Regency. Wallpapers that bring the outdoors inside with *trompe l'oeil*, and even handpainted murals, are also used

ABOVE: This dual-purpose hall belonging to interior designer David Hare is furnished with a small table that can be used for meals. On the table is a Sousani embroidered cloth which has been placed over two other pieces of antique textile, a stone plate of fruit, a witch ball and an Eastern coffee pot. On the wall is a portrait of one of Hare's ancestors.

ABOVE: This hall in a London flat designed by Racheline Nahon has an elegant appeal, with its flattering pinky beige coloring and polished marble floor. The owner collects contemporary paintings and sculpture. The drawing of a man in a Phrygian-style hat was a student work; the sculpture below it is by Malcolm Martin, and the three plates on the wall are by Stephanie Bergman.

in hallways. In wealthier town houses, hallways can be very grand, with polished marble floors. Variations on the classic black-and-white checkerboard marble floor have been in fashion since the 18th century. Light-hearted imitations come in the form of painted wood floors or floorcloths (the forerunner of late 19th-century linoleum), dating from the 18th and 19th century. The polished wood parquet floors found in the hallways of apartments converted from upper-middle-class terrace houses were usually once part of a formal drawing or dining room. The hall proper would have been floored in marble or tile, to take the brunt of wear. Strips of narrow, woven, hard-wearing carpet or drugget (a coarse, durable cloth) were laid in some long hall passages from the 19th century, changing to bare or painted boards behind the "green door." Today's halls often use a form of sisal as an alternative to carpet.

When the Arts and Crafts movement began, in the late 19th century, its interest in reviving English vernacular architecture led to halls that were large, welcoming rooms rather than passages. In upper-class houses these were known as "lounge halls" and provided all-purpose rooms where families and their guests would gather for a drink before dinner. Such halls, which were fashionable in both town and country houses, usually had a large fireplace set into an inglenook, a generous staircase, and an upper landing from which to survey the scene. They derived from the medieval "great hall" and their landings recalled the earlier minstrels' galleries. Lounge halls later became an ideal stage set for London farces in the early decades of the 20th century – especially because they had plenty of doors for exits and entrances.

The entrance hall at the newly restored Eltham Palace (opposite) is a Moderne take on the Edwardian "lounge hall." On the carpet centered under the domed roof, stripes leading from the central motifs indicate three entrances. Other service doors are concealed in the curved wood walls, while two staircases slope up to the bedroom floor. The Moderne style was a softer, more streamlined development of the Jazz Age Art Deco style of the 1920s, reflecting "The Indecisive Decade," as fashion editor Madge Garland described the 1930s. Though Art Deco was too hard-edged-chic to be at ease in England, a few daring people took it up expensively and in a particularly English idiom, such as Stephen and Virginia Courtauld in their 1937 addition to Eltham Palace, the boyhood home of Henry VIII. The Courtaulds' palace was designed in pure Ocean Liner Moderne, not least because its services echoed those of the Cunard Line's *Queen Mary*, which made its maiden voyage in 1936. In both, loudspeaker systems broadcast music in selected areas. Other *dernier cri* design elements they shared included plaster reliefs, abstract-pattern carpets, paneled interiors, decorative leather or painted maps and inlaid-wood scenes used as murals, electric clocks, built-in furniture and telephones linked to an internal exchange.

The Pantheon-esque dome of light at Eltham Palace is also not typical of most entrance halls. Before the advent of gaslight (widespread in the 1870s) and electricity (introduced in the 1880s), few halls were lit. Front doors in the 18th century had beautifully proportioned fanlights to help bring in light, while, in the 19th century, the top half of front doors were made of glass and side lights were introduced. Chain-hung lantern lights or small variations on the chandelier are often used today. Where the stairs surround a well, a chain may be as long as three storeys, with a separate light fixture for each landing.

DRAWING ROOMS

THE TERM "DRAWING ROOM" DERIVES from "withdrawing room," a chamber that developed in the medieval period, smaller than the communal great hall, to which the lord and his family and close friends would withdraw for privacy. Nowadays, the term hints at polite formality. In today's more relaxed households, the very English term "sitting room" – seldom used in America – sounds less pretentious. Sitting rooms that get good early light are sometimes called "morning rooms" and would have been used in the early 19th century by gentlemen and later by ladies of leisure to write letters and do embroidery. The old-fashioned term for a drawing room was the "parlor", from the French "*parler*," to talk. Unlike today's drawing room, a parlor in the early 19th century usually had a small, central table at which to sit and sew, play cards, have tea, or talk. Chairs were upright, encouraging good posture. Only the daringly stylish reclined on a récamier, a Regency variation of the settee, as on a daybed. Another term, of unaccountable etymology, is "lounge," but this word has commercial connotations, suggesting a hotel or an airport, and it also suggests laziness. The all-purpose transatlantic term "living room" is probably the one most frequently used because it is particularly appropriate for a room where people gather to talk, read, listen to music, play games, watch television, and entertain. It may also include a kitchen. A new contender is the "family room," which tends to be unsophisticated because it has to be child-friendly.

Certain types of drawing room are the most sumptuously decorated room in a house. Following a taste developed in the 18th century, these employ large amounts of fabric for upholstery and elaborate lined and interlined curtains, with swagged pelmets and complex tie-backs, dressed up with passementerie. Blinds and sheer curtains were probably introduced earlier, in the 17th century, and are still in frequent use today. Both allow light through while maintaining privacy. Sheer fabric and other simple curtains can also soften the appearance of a window frame. Window curtains in the 17th century, if they were used at all, were utilitarian, without pelmets and rarely in pairs. They were made of a thin, silk, taffeta-like fabric and acted as sun blinds. It was not until the 18th century that "chites" from India, now called "chintz" and fabric also known as "painted calico," began to be fashionable, for both clothing and furnishing fabric. It was at this point that English curtains, inspired by French upholsterers, became elaborate.

Both the expansion of the British Empire and the establishment of the British Raj under Queen Victoria, which placed India as the "jewel in the crown," encouraged the adoption of exotic styles. (The words "settee" and "bungalow" are both Indian.) The fashion for animal-skin rugs dates from the hunting expeditions of the British Raj, prompting the quip: "Would you like to sin with Elinor Glyn on a tiger skin or would you prefer to err with her on some other fur?" As Britain grew to be the Empire on which the sun never set, artifacts were imported and incorporated into house decoration. Pampas grass filled huge vases, while tribal masks and carved headrests reflected an interest in the so-called "primitive," which was echoed in the Art Deco movement.

The diaries of Lady Mary Wortley Montagu, the writings of Sir Richard Burton, Lawrence of Arabia, Lesley Blanche, and Freya Stark, all reflect the way the English have been attracted by the desert, ever since travel became possible to these remote places in the 18th century. The English love affair with the Middle East

is still with us today in the form of oriental rugs, antique textiles, and intricate tile work, creating interiors alive with color, pattern, and material richness. The sofa, divan, and ottoman are all Arabian in origin.

The upholstered settee was introduced in the Jacobean period (1603–25), but it was only in the second half of the 18th century that the tufted sofa made an appearance, becoming generally popular by the mid-19th century. These sofas were heavily padded with horsehair and tow, held in place with buttons, leather strips, or ribbon bows. Sofa hems began to be elaborate, with swags of fabric and heavy bullion fringe. Variations on this type of sofa, whether tufted or plain, with or without a removable seat and back cushions, are now a staple of most drawing rooms. In front of this stands a coffee table, which originated as an early 20th-century flirtation with orientalism, but now seems indispensable for stacking books.

ABOVE: The library of Alidad Mahloudji's Mayfair apartment is English in its eclecticism, the mèlange of patterns and furniture pulled together by the use of red. The fabric on the central ottoman reveals Alidad's previous work as a specialist in Islamic art and textiles at Sotheby's. It is tied with heavy cord.

ABOVE: The late Geoffrey Bennison, whose sitting room is shown here, was an antiques dealer and purveyor of highly distinctive documentary decorative fabrics. His excellent eye and intellectual style made him adept at assembling antiques in unexpected groupings. The upholstered furniture is covered with a Bennison print that has the tea-dipped look so prevalent in a certain type of English room.

RIGHT: This grandiose sitting room is an example of the English room heightened into fantasy. Assembled with passion, energy, and imagination, this parlor, one of ten rooms in Dennis Severs's restored 1724 house, was opened to the public in the 1990s, an experience considered one of the wonders of burgeoning, artistic Spitalfields. The Grinling Gibbons-esque gilded nut swags that flank the mantelpiece look genuine, but were contrived from chicken wire, Polyfilla, carved wood and plastic. Afternoon tea, set on the pedestal table, became a fashionable light meal in the 18th century, starting an English tradition. The pineapple, just introduced into England, would have been viewed as a luxury, reflecting the owner's wealth and awareness of current culinary trends.

RIGHT: Couturier David Sassoon, of Belleville-Sassoon, has a duplex in a classic 19th-century terrace house in Onslow Gardens, London. The drawing room has successfully weathered several metamorphoses, with the help of designers Nicholas Haslam and Michael Reeves. Sassoon's personal taste has also played a large part, as have the room's impeccable proportions.

In the latter half of the 18th century, the English took to pulling chairs, sofas, and "sofa tables" away from the walls and dotting them about the room or focusing them on the fireplace. The more formal French found this too casual an arrangement (being too similar to an upholsterer's shop) but the increasingly relaxed manners of the English exemplified by this change heralded the style of the 19th century.

Most English drawing rooms still have a fireplace, albeit for gas-lit fake fires, though central heating is commonplace in cities. Real fires, though cozy and comforting, are messy, while burning coal in Central London, for instance, is now forbidden, putting an end to the "pea-soup" fogs that were a regular occurrence up until the mid-20th century.

Fireplaces were moved from the middle of the room to a side wall with a chimney in the Middle Ages, and in the Tudor period became the focal point of a room. From that time on, however, fireplaces gradually diminished in size because they were more efficient by controlling smoke using flues. Grates with pierced metal fenders for burning coal were design features by the mid-18th century, though the use

LEFT: *The silver room in theatre director Rodney Archer's Spitalfields house was inspired by the original 18th-century paneling which he burnished with Dutch silver leaf, outlined in gold and surrounded by a rich cobalt blue. A witch ball c.1900 echoes the silver theme. Sitting room doors open into a library with terracotta and Etruscan red shelves designed by Patrick Handscombe.*

of coal had been considered vulgar compared to wood logs. Also during this period, ornamental firebacks came into vogue and chimney boards were used to cover the fireplace during summer. Mantelpieces were now topped by a mirror, which in a grand house might be a Chinese Chippendale confection. The Classically inspired chimney pieces of Robert Adam (1728–92) were particularly beautiful products of this century, displaying an unostentatious elegance and opulence, such as the one at Syon House (1760–69) near London, made from coloured marble with gilt details.

With the Arts and Crafts movement, fireplaces increased in size, set in inglenooks and under Tudor-esque arches, but by the 1930s and 1940s they had diminished once more, and become unobtrusive pastel tile-covered rectangles, although the family continued to gather round them until the television became the main focus. At the end of the 20th century, architect John Pawson reduced the fireplace to its utmost simplicity (see page 37). Nevertheless, in the rarefied world of *le haut décor*, a well-arranged mantelshelf, with that essential balanced asymmetry of choice objects and personal whimsy, is still considered a test of taste.

Geoffrey Bennison was known for his antiques, fabrics (especially his 19th-century documentary cretonnes, with their dipped-in-tea look), interior decoration and interest in architecture, all of which are reflected in his very English sitting room/study shown on page 26. His rooms often look like theatre sets, with an edge of accumulated grandeur in a particularly English idiom (the dilapidated feel is intentional). This room shows his skill in collecting and assembling antiques. Other English decorators with this talent included David Hicks, whose "tablescapes," dating from the late 1950s to the early 1970s, were legendary in their ability to meld disparate antiques with objects found in nature.

FAR LEFT: *This mantelpiece was found in Tite Street in a house where Oscar Wilde used to live. The once run-down Spitalfields neighborhood has gradually been discovered by architecture buffs. On the mantelshelf are pieces by artists who live in the area; the two busts are by Guy Burch and the "Weight Lifter" figure is by Margaret Proudfoot.*

*OPPOSITE: The sitting room
of an 1860 terrace house in
south London belonging to
garden designer Christopher
Masson. French doors open
onto a balcony overlooking a
back garden beyond a flourish
of wisteria and a wall of
climbing roses. The lamp base
on the c.1820 French Empire
pedestal table is made from an
Art Nouveau figure given to
Masson on his 18th birthday
by his parents. Seen lit behind
the lampshade is a painting by
Bloomsburyite Bernard
Meninsky. The cushion on the
1840s mahogany chair is
antique English needlepoint.*

The late Dennis Severs restored his 1724 house in London's Spitalfields (see page 27) to be exaggeratedly English. He wished to recreate the original atmosphere through an exacting level of historical accuracy, banning conveniences such as electricity, central heating, and a modern cooker. He peopled his house with a fictional Huguenot family of silk weavers, based on one that had lived in the house for five generations, and invited the public to a historical "happening." Sounds, such as horses' hooves, could be heard as though coming from outside, and smells – even of urine – were all part of the experience.

In Severs' 18th-century sitting room, the walls are divided with wood paneling. With the revival of Classical architecture came a division into cornice, field and dado, to be replaced in the Victorian period (1837–1901) with a division created by the dado and the picture rail. The English were the first to make flocked wallpaper, in the mid-18th century, and by the 19th century it was typically used in red tones on dining-room walls. Wallpaper as a whole was mass-produced in the mid-19th century, when other wall coverings that simulated low-relief effects were also invented. The earliest wall coverings, wall hangings, were introduced in the Norman period (1066–1154), when they were used to obscure rough walls and provide varied decoration. They were also easy to transport. As the lives of the wealthy became less peripatetic, tapestries were fixed in place with greater permanency. By the 17th century, upholsterers were responsible for the wall coverings in all but the most humble rooms and those rooms that were wood-paneled. They often used silk, brocatelle (silk reinforced with linen), wool or worsted (when woven in large patterns, this was called "dornix" in England), or, more rarely, imported velvet or plain cloth professionally – and expensively – embroidered.

When Rodney Archer, a director of drama, moved into his 1726 house in Spitalfields (see pages 30 and 31), it was far from being the fashionable place it is today. The small but elegant houses in its narrow streets had been built in the early 18th century for prosperous Huguenot silk weavers fleeing religious persecution. By the end of the 19th century, the neighborhood had deteriorated: this was the area Jack the Ripper prowled through. As Archer gradually restored the house, finding bits and pieces of the original molding stashed away in a cupboard, it took on an air of fantasy in keeping with his own theatrical background. He even found a mantelpiece that came from a house where Oscar Wilde – one of Archer's heroes – had once lived. All the painting was purposefully distressed to make it look worn.

The drawing room in the 18th-century mews house shown on page 29 started as a stable designed by William Kent. Fodder would have been dropped from the floor above to the horses stabled in this room. Converted into a double-height drawing room by Colefax & Fowler in the mid-1950s, John Fowler found and had installed the 18th-century chandelier, its long chain sleeved in silk taffeta. The generously proportioned mirror, also designed by William Kent, was found by Mrs. A.J. Heinz, the mews house owner. The silk curtains and over-swags with their large-scale tassels have been designed to accommodate the arched windows that open out to the central courtyard.

When David Green became Chairman of Colefax & Fowler, he and his wife Judy called upon one of their leading interior designers, Roger Banks-Pye, to help decorate their 1920s Arts and Crafts-influenced

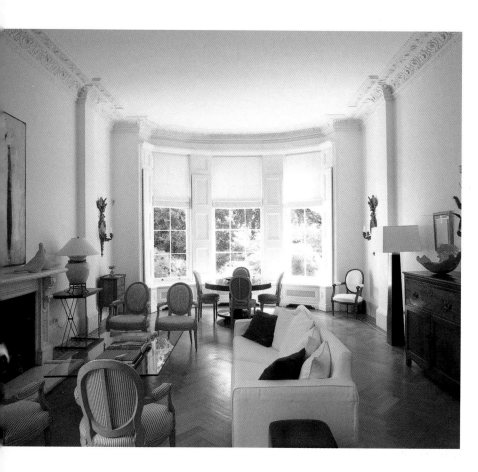

ABOVE: Roland Klein, a fashion-designer-turned-decorator, lives in an 1860 London terrace apartment where his drawing room has the luxury of looking out over a communal garden. The 18th-century French chairs came from his family but he has re-upholstered them in crisp cotton ticking stripes to give a relaxed, modern look. Brushed cotton twill covers the sofa. Cushions are canvas with leather strapping. The bowl on the sideboard was sculpted by Althea Wilson. In keeping with today's pared-down look, the bare parquet floor has been restored and polished.

RIGHT: In this sitting room belonging to David and Judy Green, the influence of the Arts and Crafts movement can be seen in the fireplace with its Tudor-esque arch set into an inglenook. All the fabrics and the carpet are from Colefax & Fowler, where David Green is the Chairman. The decorator was the late Roger Banks-Pye, a star designer at the firm. The designer's signature is shown in the paintwork which is done in three subtle shades of cream. Botanical prints reflect Judy Green's avid involvement with flowers and gardens.

ABOVE: *This loft in Hoxton London is a vast, airy space. The kitchen, office, bedroom, and bathroom have been partitioned off by white-painted walls. A central seating area includes the sofa – a vintage radiator – softened with two floor cushions. A clear plastic bubble chair suspends from the beams and can be moved at will.*

house in Hampstead (see page 35). For this, one of his last projects before his untimely death, Banks-Pye produced a traditional, supremely comfortable but relaxed interior. The Colefax influence can be seen in the simple checked and striped fabrics and the antique platters set on the high mantel.

As living in central London became increasingly expensive towards the end of the 20th century, warehouses in dock areas and commercial districts were rejuvenated. Their conversion represented a new take on the post-Second World War trend for open-plan houses, in which one room melded into another. In these warehouse properties, the living room incorporates a sitting area, dining room, and kitchen, as in the top-floor apartment owned by journalist Aurora Irvine and art director Jason Shulman in fashionable Hoxton (above). This loft building was originally used for making bricks and pots, then

became a warehouse, but it has now been divided into living and working spaces. Decoration here is raffish and contemporary: a mirrored bathroom door that collapsed has been recycled into a dining table.

Architect John Pawson made his name in the 1980s and 1990s by designing spaces and houses unlike anything seen before. His aesthetic is the International Style of the 20th century, but his yearning for simplicity is as palpable as Marie Antoinette's when she created her *Hameau* at Versailles – and well-nigh as expensive. Though cool, chic, and angular, a traditional English aspect is apparent in the inclusion of a fireplace – no longer necessary for heat – in the living room of his own turn-of-the-millennium house (above). This is the archetypal modern architect's room, with ingenious furnishings, an innate suspicion of color, and a loathing of clutter.

ABOVE: In the center of this minimal living room in John Pawson's London house is a sofa with a back ledge that forms a desk. The floor, plus a bench running along one wall, are of fossil-filled Italian lecce limestone. Books, television and even photographs are hidden away behind a wall of cupboards.

DINING ROOMS

A CENTURY AGO, THE DINING ROOM was used by English middle-class families for every meal. The husband worked nearby, the children walked to school, and they all came home for midday dinner, the main meal of the day. Only servants – who were considered working class – ate in the kitchen. Now, in our bustling city lives, lunch is often taken on the run and the dining room is only used intermittently, for evening dinner parties, fancy luncheons, and family get-togethers during holidays or on festive occasions.

Rooms set aside simply for dining are a comparatively recent development in English interiors. Until the 18th century, eating and sleeping often took place in the same room, where informal repasts might be set at small tables. Large gatherings took place in a hall, where a long board was rested on trestles and covered with a cloth, giving rise to such expressions as "chairman of the board," for the

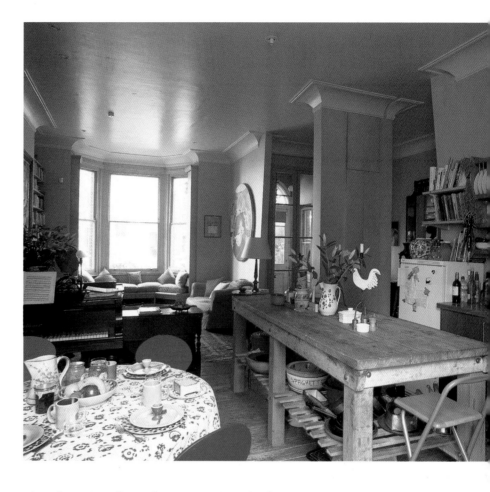

LEFT: An air of relaxation combined with formality is achieved in this dining room in a house in Hampstead, London. The old oak table is surrounded by chairs copied from a single 18th-century chair found by the interior designer, the late Roger Banks-Pye. The informal effect is helped by the choice of crisp brown-and-white "Eaton Check" from Colefax & Fowler as the main upholstery fabric. Other fabrics from the same firm can be seen used in the sitting room beyond.

person who sat at the head of the table on a chair (rather than a bench), and "groaning board," for a table that creaked when weighed down with food. Even cup-boards were pieces of furniture that could be temporarily dismantled. The ascendancy of the superb furniture designers of the 18th century meant that splendid, permanent dining-room tables were produced. Sets of matching chairs to surround them have never been bettered for looks or comfort. To accommodate them, dining rooms became essential. These rooms often had magnificent architectural details such as pillars, pilasters, niches, dados, and crown molding.

In the early 18th century, during the reign of George I (1714–27), a heavy, Baroque style was fashionable in dining-room furniture. (The word "Baroque" is probably derived from the Portuguese "*barocco*," meaning an imperfect or grotesque pearl.) The cup-board and dresser now became a side table and by 1800 this was known as a "sideboard." Elaborate, curved, and bulbous carving appeared on chairs with cabriole legs, each with a lion's head or human mask at the knee and terminating in a ball-and-claw foot. The shell motif was especially fashionable, and walnut was a favourite wood.

By the middle of the 18th century, furniture design was dominated by Thomas Chippendale, whose preferred wood was mahogany. Dining-room chairs became lighter, and the carving better executed and more intricate. Chairs could be found in three basic styles: Gothic, Rococo, and Chinese. By the end of the century, golden-coloured satinwood had become stylish, and inlay and marquetry were popular as decoration. Chairs became lighter again, with tapering legs. George Hepplewhite is best remembered from this period for his shield- and oval-backed chairs, and Thomas Sheraton for his

ABOVE: This row house in Kilburn, north London, was found in a pre-war time warp, having been owned by the same family since it was built in 1900. To create an open-plan dining/living room/kitchen, the new owner Christopher Sykes altered structural details, adding the wide pillar between the kitchen and hall area.

RIGHT: This London dining room belonging to interior designer Alidad is used for formal dinner parties and the owner aims for an over-the-top effect of sumptuous glamor. The trompe-l'oeil *ceiling was formed from patterns painted on squares of wood by the artist in his studio, then assembled in situ. On the walls, Islamic-looking flowers, peaches. pomegranates and vines are colorfully painted and gilded on squares of tooled leather, a form of wall decoration that harks back to 17th-century Europe. Chairs are upholstered in cut velvet and embellished with braid. Despite the opulence, the Minton plates and starched white napkins give a hint of English decorum.*

BELOW: Some of the most charming dining areas are those set in libraries. In this room, which belonged to poet Stephen Spender, rows of books are the perfect backdrop to an intimate meal for three. A portrait of the poet Christopher Isherwood hangs on the front of the bookshelf, a typical device used in English decorating.

apparently even more fragile chairs, which were often decorated with inlay or refined painting, a foretaste of the Regency chairs to come. These drew on Greek, Roman, and Egyptian sources, including an adaptation of the Greek *klismos* shape: a back rail with sides sweeping to the front then curving to the floor in a sickle shape, or with arms scrolled forward from the back rail to the seat.

Cutlery reached a high standard of design in the 18th century, and is still the benchmark by which silverware is judged, for its Classical style, proportions, and ease of use. Far more silverware was manufactured during this period than in previous centuries. For those who could not afford solid silver, Old Sheffield Plate, a silver coating on a copper base, was an alternative for cutlery and for tea and coffee sets, until electroplating was introduced in the 1840s. Regency silverware, though more delicate than Georgian pieces, was still beautifully designed, with simple fluting, beadwork, and engraved vine leaves. After the mid-19th century, silverware became over-ostentatious, heavy, and badly proportioned, and therefore less comfortable to use, although it remained popular, especially at London's increasingly opulent dinner tables, which continued to serve many courses right up to the Second World War.

Josiah Wedgwood is the best-known potter of the late 18th century. A great promoter of the neo-Classical style – his jasperware incorporated white bas-relief figures on a coloured ground – he also helped to create a wider market for luxury goods. English porcelain factories flourished at this time, producing high-quality products that are now much collected, including Minton, Worcester, and Coalport. In the Victorian period, china designs, like silverware, became highly elaborate, and from then on, because of industrialization, their quality declined.

By the 19th century, most households, except for the servant class, had a dining room, plus a cook, and a maid (or a butler for the wealthy) to bring food from the kitchen. If the kitchen was below stairs, a dumb waiter on a pulley brought the food up to be served. Dining rooms gradually became cluttered with side tables, whatnots, and tiered stands. The cult of the well-set table was taken up by the wives of the newly wealthy industrialists: domed silver entrée dishes, wine coolers, special serving implements for food such as peas – or even ice cream – knife rests, serviette rings, or napkins folded into fancy shapes, graced the dining rooms of those craving respectability. The First World War put an end to such elaborate arrangements, however. Many servants left to fight in the war or to work in factories, which meant that wives were obliged to learn how to cook. Labor-saving devices were introduced, such as a hatch in the wall between the kitchen and the dining room through which to push food, a feature still found in smaller English houses. Tables were still covered with white cloths but, by the 1920s, colored napery was making an appearance. Individual place mats were taken up by the smart set in the 1930s. Now used universally in town, place mats can be found made of straw, linen, cork, rubber, fabric, mirror glass, or in chic plastic versions.

Around the 1900s, city boroughs developed rows of middle- and working-class houses. Each house had a separate sitting room and dining room – and the kitchen was definitely a woman's place. The dining/living room/kitchen shown on page 39 was originally designed in this format, but the new owner, Christopher Sykes, found the arrangement outdated for today's city life. Having previously lived in

houses with formal dining rooms, he, along with many others, found that they were seldom used except for entertaining. The ground floor was therefore gutted and redesigned to suit a more contemporary lifestyle. The long kitchen table, which once belonged to a Yorkshire butcher, was given legs and under-shelves, creating a perfect work island – a modern kitchen concept – from a vintage piece of furniture.

Lack of space is a major concern in town apartments. Small flats cannot accommodate separate dining rooms and so eating areas often have to be created, whether in an entrance hall, the corner of a drawing room, fitted into a kitchen, or wedged for special occasions into an infrequently used guest room. Dining rooms squeezed into intimate, candlelit spaces have a romantic quality, a town version of the small banqueting houses of country follies. They can have brilliant jewel-box-like interiors with murals, fantastic wallpaper, fabric-covered walls, and tented ceilings. Some of the most congenial dining rooms are in libraries, such as the library dining room in Sir John Soane's Museum in London (built in 1812–13), or the more intimate version that belonged to the late poet Sir Stephen Spender (see page 40).

ABOVE: An informal repast laid out in Celia Lyttleton's dining room reflects her unique sense of color. Anchored by bare floorboards painted pale aqua, the walls have been textured in yellow with a darker ochre high dado echoing a painted detail on the crown molding. The bronzed fireplace surround reflects the warm, golden light.

In the 1980s, if there were more guests than one table could comfortably hold, two or more tables became fashionable. For very large gatherings, a dining room table becomes a spectacular buffet with guests standing or finding their own seating all over the apartment or house.

Dining rooms in town are used mostly in the evening, so good lighting is vital. In the 18th century, they were lit by candles, set in chandeliers, candelabra, wall-sconces, candlestands made of gilded wood or gesso, or in candlesticks. The use of mirrors helped to increase the light, as did reflections from the glass drops on chandeliers, which became popular in the late Georgian period. Today there are many choices, from glittering 18th-century crystal chandeliers, either wired for electricity or retaining candles, to New Age versions such as the twisted-wire concoctions designed by Seth Stein; from ornate Edwardianesque silk shades dripping with beaded fringes to simple concealed spots; from traditional candelabra and candlesticks to those designed by Jason Shulman, which balance on the edge of the table. Alidad Mahloudji, designer of the dining room shown on page 41, combines the mystery of the Middle East with

the decorum of the English. His Mayfair dining room is a night-time room, lit only by candles that randomly catch the glint of gilt on walls and ceiling. By contrast, Celia Lyttleton's dining room (see page 43) shows simple, modern wood and metal chairs surrounding a glass-topped table. The effect echoes today's relaxed way of life in an entirely personal way.

In 1995, architect Seth Stein adapted a mews house and courtyard in Kensington, London, to create a U-shaped house tailored to the needs of his young family. Glass walls on the interior of the U-formation help him and his wife to keep an eye on their young children while giving them plenty of space to zoom around, as though they were in a loft space. One stem of the U-shape includes an open-plan kitchen and eating area with a central island dividing the space lengthways.

Life in the city is competitive, with hosts vying for the most inventive ideas. Sometimes professional designers are called in to create an effect. No matter how impressive the scene as you enter, it is no longer quite so important once the guests are seated because they themselves – if well selected – become the drama.

ABOVE: Architect Seth Stein designed this open-plan space in a U-shape surrounding a minimal garden. Reflecting modern living in England, the kitchen area with its central work island overlooks an informal eating area. Stein himself does not like accumulating objects but his children do, so their toys are stored in the cardboard igloo seen at the far end of the room.

back rooms

kitchens,
work *rooms* &
studies

LEFT: When decorator Melissa Wyndham's clients inherited this kitchen from previous owners, it was unfortunately done up in ugly dragged peach paint. They decided to keep the bones of the kitchen intact, and a compromise was reached by introducing more appealing colors and changing the work top.

ABOVE: In West House, where Professor Bernard Nevill lives, the library/drawing room bookcases were designed by Henry Whitaker for the Conservative Club. The library ladders came from the old Times building. Enjoying the "swagger of large-scale furniture," Nevill has deep-seated Howard sofas, heavy tapestry curtains and a vintage gramophone from the Monkey Club, used to help the girls learn typing.

KITCHENS

Up until the Stuart period, the kitchen in a large house would have been almost the same in the town and the country. By 1660, however, such huge kitchens had been somewhat reduced in size, especially in towns, and cooking – roasting, baking and boiling – was more likely to be done over a coal fire. The spit, which was once turned by a boy, or a dog in a cage, was now operated by a clockwork jack.

By the early 18th century, kitchens had plain plaster walls and ceilings, stone floors, and sinks, which were shallow stone or earthenware troughs. Water had to be hand-pumped outside, while hot water was heated in a cauldron hung over the fire. Kitchen furniture included a dresser, one or more cupboards, a table and a larder. Some houses also had a separate china room and a scullery. By the end of the century, cast-iron ranges would have been installed in a few sophisticated houses. Known as "kitcheners", these grew in number until, by the mid-19th century, they were found in all but the lowliest town houses. Smaller versions were used as the main method of cooking until well into the 20th century, but were now powered by gas. Electric cookers did not become popular until after 1918.

Kitchens in the late 19th and early 20th century were even smaller, especially in middle-income homes in town. They were nearer to the dining room and had a scullery attached, often with a red quarry-tiled floor. The scullery, which held the sink, now had running water, while above the fireplace was a copper used to heat water for washing. These back rooms, found at the end of the hall passage, were the domain of the cook and little attention was paid to their looks. The walls were still painted white, often with a water-based paint called "distemper," and linoleum covered the floors. Refrigeration was rarely found in town houses until after the Second World War: food was kept on a stone slab in the larder or pantry.

Compared to France, considered the most sophisticated country for haute cuisine, English food was anything but gourmet. Despite Mrs. Beeton's famous *Book of Household Management*, with its abundant recipes, in Britain food was generally regarded as fodder. "Fancy French food" was not encouraged, and English children were taught that it was rude to discuss food at the table. Nowadays, good food and cooking have become legitimate topics. Full-time cooks exist in private houses but are rare, and the battery of servants that used to operate out of sight is non-existent. In a society with little full-time help, cooking with or in front of guests is accepted as part of the entertainment. A substantial bar with stools or an island with a built-in sink may divide the cooking area from the living room and may also be used as a sideboard or dining table. Home owners have become skilled cooks and enjoy cooking for family and friends as a fashionable pursuit. Kitchens are now meant to be seen and are decorated accordingly, with the kitchen area reflecting the owner's taste and personality. Today a kitchen is revamped every 30 years or so, usually at ruinous expense.

The old-fashioned kitchen has a stylish appeal to those who still use with pleasure their grandmother's smooth stone pestle and mortar or an antique family spice box – vintage culinary items more likely to be found in antique shops. Though it appears to be the cluttered look carried to its ultimate degree, artist Richard Beer deliberately preserves an outdated kitchen in his house in Regent's Park, London. His kitchen (opposite) has remained more or less the same since the 1950s. He still uses the same stove – now converted

to North Sea gas — that he bought from friends in 1955 and which they had acquired in the 1940s. What is more, he has never cleaned the oven and so it is totally black inside which, he avers, makes life much easier. Though small, the kitchen is also used as a dining room and can seat six at a pinch. One work table is a vintage washstand from a bedroom. Two of the tables cost seven shillings and sixpence (just over $1) each. They are covered in American cloth (the old-fashioned, very English name for a type of pre-vinyl oil cloth) brought in the 1960s from Greece. Efficiency is less of a priority than quirky visual effects. The light bulb is enclosed within the type of red plastic net that usually holds supermarket vegetables, because Beer likes the look of it. There is a vintage EasyWork cabinet from the 1930s and a collection of labeled tins on the wall, along with a big factory clock with a face on both sides from the Port de Montreuil in France.

ABOVE: The English have been collectors since the 17th century. A cluster of things, great and small, overflow in Richard Beer's kitchen. Every object tells a story: trompe-l'oeil artist Judith Downie painted the fireplace; the lamp over the stove is a flour filter; the candlesticks are Moroccan, made from old sardine tins.

David Edgel and Maria Marinho's cutting-edge kitchen (see page 53) is the opposite of Dick Beer's extraordinary hodgepodge of culled bits and pieces. Both rooms reflect their owners' differing attitudes. Assembled all-of-a-piece by Edgel, a product designer, this brand-new kitchen in their loft in the Clerkenwell district of London has stainless steel counters, sinks, and a stove running along one wall.

The affluence of the last decades of the 20th century introduced the fashionable trophy kitchen. Instead of the movable kitchen work table of the past, a permanent central island with built-in appliances and overhead lights provides a counter at which to work and eat. In these kitchens, sinks are set into granite counters, racks of gleaming pans hang above, wall cupboards house quantities of china and glass, and double-door refrigerators hold fresh and frozen food – and even cut flowers. Curtains hang at the windows and match seat

LEFT: The kitchen in Celia Lyttleton's house looks cool and restful due to the pale eau-de-nil walls, the slightly deeper tone of the painted floorboards, and the deep aquamarine of the cupboards and shelves.

RIGHT: The kitchen in a house where photographer Christopher Sykes used to live in London shows clear yellow walls bordered by a blue design of coffee pots, teapots and cups. This is a favorite scheme and similar to the kitchen in his country house in Yorkshire. Overhead, blue glassed-in cupboards are arched and the shape is echoed in the blue plywood cupboard doors below the sink counter. His young children could be easily watched when playing in the room off the kitchen. Steps lead down to a conservatory dining room. An avid (and somewhat indiscriminate) collector of pigs, these can be seen on the walls, on the shelves, and even the chopping board is shaped like a pig.

pad covers on banquettes against the walls. Some kitchens are even expensively wallpapered. Nearby, a separate utility room has washing apparatus and all the tools and cleaning equipment needed to keep a modern home running efficiently. The emphasis on a big, new kitchen has given rise to English kitchen specialists such as Smallbone of Devizes, Christians, and Mark Wilkinson – businesses that developed from skilled cabinet workshops in the west of England. These companies now globally export elaborate modern kitchens with neo-traditional detailing, glass-fronted cupboards, paneling, and dentil molding.

As early as 1792, John Soane's first house at No. 12 Lincoln's Inn Fields, London, included a "breakfast parlor," though it was used as an informal dining room and a library. In the latter half of the 20th century, the kitchen area in largish houses began to include a breakfast room, used by the family far more frequently than a formal dining room. This is where adults have their morning coffee and read the newspapers before heading off to work, where children have breakfast before going to school, and where lunch is eaten. A breakfast room lends itself to modest decoration: simple curtains, walls decorated with collections of china, padded fabric-covered banquettes or sturdy chairs, and an unpretentious wood or painted table.

More often than not, however, space is at a premium in the city. Older houses that have been adapted into small flats often have tiny kitchens because they have been concocted out of rooms that originally had other uses. There may be space for no more than one or two people, but these kitchens are perfect for those who prefer not to be distracted when cooking. Small kitchens can be efficient if well planned. Of all the rooms in the house, the kitchen is the one that benefits the most from a specialist space planner rather than an interior designer.

RIGHT: When designing this kitchen space in a renovated Clerkenwell loft, designer David Edgel turned to TTC Cheltenham Caterings Solutions who specialize in equipment for restaurants and commercial kitchens. This unit was made to Edgel's specifications and was so successful that the firm wanted him to design for them. The stainless steel movable island is used as a work space or a table. Stainless steel is a practical, easy-to-clean, non-rusting material that has been used throughout the 20th century. It became prominent in the High-Tech boom of the late 1970s, but was never as popular as it became at the end of the century.

LEFT: On a landing in Richard Beer's house, the door to his studio is clearly and jokily marked ATELIER. Above a protruding shelf is a letter box from France decorated with Mexican piñata-covering paper, while paper roses made by a friend collect a welcome patina of dust.

LEFT: Inside artist Richard Beer's studio, concocted from a bedroom on the second floor of his Regent's Park house, a large mirror helps to bring light into the room. At any given time, several of his paintings will be in progress — Grenada with palm trees, a water scene in Siena, a man sitting outside a place where Beer once stayed in Ronda.

THE TERM "WORK ROOMS" HERE REFERS TO rooms that have been converted into a working area of a specific nature, such as studios, offices, or sewing rooms. Large town houses in the 18th and 19th century had a butler's or a housekeeper's room that would, in some ways, have been equivalent to today's work rooms. From the 17th century onward, artists frequently had a studio in their houses or in a separate building nearby, set in the garden. Private dressmakers throughout the 19th and much of the 20th century had rooms set aside at home for their work, which clients would visit, though in a large household they would have lived as one of the staff. Up until the 1930s, it was also fairly common for a dressmaker to stay for a few days with a family, measuring for new clothes and even cutting loose covers for furniture, where she would be given a temporary work room.

For those who sew at home today, a work room is a boon as otherwise fabric has to be cut on the floor or the dining-room table. A good-sized foldaway table is essential, as are shelves, cupboards, or

WORK ROOMS

RIGHT: *Product designer David Edgel keeps his office simple and slick. The glass-topped desk holds business paraphernalia plus his iMac computer – a prerequisite of contemporary office chic. A black leather chair and tufted couch are the main pieces of furniture. The only whimsy is in the fireplace where there is a neat rectangle of candles which can be lit to create mood when needed.*

ABOVE: Photographer Christopher Sykes's office, in a house where he used to live, shows his heavy-duty typewriter, alongside the now essential computer, fax and phone. The shelves of books include some for which Sykes did the photography, some which he has written, and others which he uses for reference. The photographs of Sykes holding his son as an infant were taken by American photographer Annie Leibovitz.

decorative boxes for fabric, threads, and sewing equipment. None of these containers has to be mundane but can be an antique or a mid-20th-century retro piece reflecting the owner's personality. For those with a knowledge of sewing, simple loose covers and curtains can be made for the room. It is then possible for a practical sewing room to double as an extra sitting room.

Today a growing number of people work at home. If they spend all day and often much of the evening at work, their surroundings and the way they look become vital. A work room's decoration reflects the owner's equipment, needs, and career. A form-follows-function sensibility combined with personal expression makes these rooms fascinating – a glimpse into someone's mind, straddling the space between public and private life, whether the room itself is minimal or messy.

A painting studio reflects the artist, whether it is at the back of the house, in a loft or an attic, or in a woodshed in the back garden. Traditional artists demand a good north light, but modernists may prefer completely artificial light. Some studios exude the evocative smell of turpentine, others the easy-clean blandness of acrylics. Tools of the trade may include paints, brushes, pastels, and charcoal, in the traditional manner, but can also incorporate state-of-the-art computer software.

Art studios range from the Bohemian to the high tech. In the late 18th century, artists such as William Blake gave rise to the Romantic idea of the isolated, creative genius, needing a private space in order to create; and figures such as Benjamin Robert Haydon fostered images of the raffish artist pursuing an irregular lifestyle. Most of England's Pre-Raphaelites lived in respectable upper-middle-class town houses, though this did not prevent them from leading scandalous lives.

Members of the Bloomsbury Group, in the early 20th century, also came from prosperous backgrounds. Composed of writers, artists, musicians, and original thinkers, the group's relationships were deeply entangled. The sister of writer Virginia Woolf, Vanessa Bell, lived with the artist Duncan Grant; their house, Charleston Manor, is a triumph of personal decoration and has become a Mecca for design aficionados. The Omega workshops, founded by Roger Fry in 1913, which produced furniture and textiles designed by Bell and Grant, were in this same loving-hands, splash-on-the-paint creative vein, though time has revealed that the workmanship often left something to be desired.

Artists of the latter half of the 20th century, and today, come from all walks of life, though to establish their presence and credibility they tend to gather in a major city where they will find a gallery and be

RIGHT: *This room in Brian Godbold's North London apartment works as a sitting room and small studio. The tailor's dummy is a reminder of his long career as a fashion design director. Some of his favorite African pots and other sculptural pieces sit on the bureau. The framed pictures of animals are lithographic advertisements for different types of fur found in the south of France.*

noticed. Many take pride in being professional and businesslike, working closely with assistants and agents. They decorate their homes with a creative and personal flair that bypasses or anticipates trends.

A lifetime's accumulation of personal ephemera surrounds painter Richard Beer. The conglomeration of artifacts on the landing door leading to his studio (see page 54) is typical of the way in which his Regent's Park house has gradually been furnished. A true recycler of junk, he acquired from a neighbor a small shelf that was about to be thrown out. He painted and distressed the shelf and was wandering up and down his house with it in his hand when he stopped at this door and decided that it was the only place for it. The shelf reminded him of those found in provincial ticket offices that used to have little shutters that opened and closed. Next to the door, on either side of a shell-framed mirror, are favorite pictures reflecting his buoyant personality and frequent travels, including two drawings by the French neo-Impressionist Georges Seurat of women in bustles, Beer's favorite shape. The wood finials came from Florence, the bookshelves from the local market. Like the products of the Charlestonites, the coterie around Vanessa Bell and Duncan Grant, Beer's work is partly decorative, but also includes landscapes, cityscapes, and theatre sets. Inside his studio (see page 55), paintings in progress reflect his travels around the Mediterranean.

Photographer Christopher Sykes's office work space (see page 56) is an unusual, but perhaps quintessentially English, combination. Part bedroom, part sitting room, and part studio, on the top floor of a London town house and lit by skylights, the space rambles around a corner to a desk complete with shelves for slides and transparencies, packed together and giving an overall effect of organized clutter.

At the opposite end of the scale is the 21st-century office that belongs to designer David Edgel, a modernist who combines art, research, and financial acumen. Artistic clutter is not his style. He works with a computer and a clear desk. Caught up in "dot commerce," many of the young and ambitious are running internet businesses from a single room in their home. The furnishings in these rooms have for the most part focused on what the computer can do. The main area consists of a "work station," usually a table loaded with electronic equipment in varying shades of plain vanilla, though there is now some serious interest in the way computers and their components look. For instance, the translucent colors of iMacs, with their fruit names – lime, blueberry, grape, strawberry, and tangerine – may well ensure that they, like antique easels and cameras, become collectors' items some years hence.

Product designer David Edgel and painter Maria Marinho moved to Clerkenwell in London before it became fashionable in the 1990s. Their loft building stands on the site of a row of artisans' houses that were replaced in the 19th century by a storage warehouse. In the early 20th century, the building was a gramophone needle factory, but at the end of the century it was converted into three properties. Edgel and Marinho took the raw space of one floor and divided it up according to their own design (see page 61). Marinho uses part of the area as her studio, while a central expanse forms the sitting room, defined by a sisal carpet. A glass table surrounded by metal-framed bentwood chairs creates the dining area. An all-purpose room, it is used for both work and play.

STUDIES ARE PRIVATE WORK ROOMS, often with a scholarly demeanor. They are distantly related to the Renaissance *studiolo*, a room where men and women in the ruling families could display their culture and learning through fabulous works of art, though these rooms were intended as a public display of status rather than an intellectual retreat. In the grander English houses of the 17th century, a small room was often set aside as a study, containing bookcases, a table, and a reading stand. In France, such rooms might be part of an apartment, or an adjunct to a library, and were often decorated in quite a glamorous style, but in England they were considered less public and remained part of the gentleman's preserve until the latter half of the 20th century. The diarist Samuel Pepys purportedly kept his writing paper locked in his study so that even his wife had no access to it.

STUDIES

ABOVE: This huge living/ working/kitchen/dining room belonging to designer David Edgel and artist Maria Marinho was painted in three slightly differing shades of off-white to subtly delineate the different areas. Marinho's studio space is in the foreground. The kitchen lies along one wall, and the dining area can be seen in the far corner. Metal overhead lights are from the Conran shop.

LEFT: Celia Lyttleton's attractive, uncluttered attic studio at the top of her house is full of endlessly surprising color combinations. Blue-stained rafters and a floor painted with blue stripes contrast with walls that are mottled dull yellow. The skirting boards are blue to match the banisters. A window on the staircase has a blue and yellow hand-dyed curtain. The ladder can be let down so one can reach the trap door opening in the ceiling. Adding a light touch are the bent wire chair and bench, and the work table with curved legs. Light streams in from an attic window, which has white-on-white sheer embroidered curtains.

upstairs

landings, bedrooms
& bathrooms

ABOVE: Head of Bellville-Sassoon, David Sassoon's bandbox-neat little bathroom has a Scottish theme. The plaid walls, on which circular plaques are hung, are edged with tartan ribbon. The mirror over the sink reflects a neo-Classical statuette of a lady gracefully reclining on a day bed.

LEFT: This Moderne bedroom at Eltham Palace was designed for Virginia Courtauld by her friend, the flamboyant Italian playboy designer Peter Malacrida who was then working for the English decorating firm White Allom. The curved walls are lined with maple flexwood, a fashionable product at the time which consists of a thin veneer backed with paper that could be hung like wallpaper.

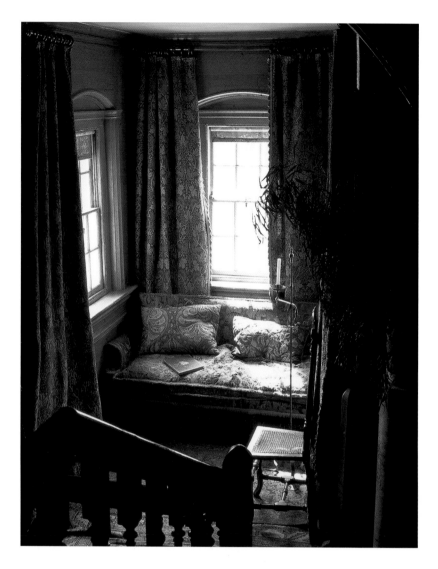

LEFT: Professor Bernard Nevill's 1868 Arts-and-Crafts house in Chelsea was designed by Philip Webb for his friend, the architectural watercolorist G. P. Boyce. The curtains are Merton Abbey pure wool damask designs called Tulip and Rose and they still bear the labels of Morris & Company when it operated in Oxford Street. The 17th-century sofa by the window is covered with 17th-century tapestry. Elizabethan stump work covers one of the cushions, and the other is covered in 19th-century Ottoman woven wool. The Charles II fruitwood chair is one of six; the rest are scattered through the house.

RIGHT: Leading up from the flagstoned hall of David and Julia Green's 1920s house in Hampstead is this half-landing. On either side of a niche that holds a Portuguese settee are antique mirrors that bring in light and an illusion of space. This was helped by designer Roger Banks-Pye's insistence on lightening the hall area by painting the walls a whitened beige and liming the oak paneling and stairs. The seat pad and cushions are covered in Colefax & Fowler fabric.

LANDINGS

STONE STAIRCASES LEADING TO THE TOP of Norman and medieval castles spiraled around a central column called a newel post and had masonry walls. Box staircases in Tudor and Jacobean houses were entered through a door at the top and bottom, and enclosed on either side with walls of wood or plaster. Gradually, however, the staircase was opened up so that one side was fixed to the wall and the other had carved or turned balusters that supported a handrail. Carved finials decorated and gave extra height to the newel post at the foot of the stairs and at each turn.

In the 18th century, banisters were made of wood, marble, stone, or wrought metal with gilded details. Grand town houses had imperial staircases open on both sides, derived from the exuberant Baroque style but given an English flavor by architects such as Sir William Chambers and Robert Adam. Steps rose from the entrance hall and divided at a half-landing before sweeping up in two flights to the main landing. Some staircases worked in reverse, separating into two flights as they curved down to the hall. Such grandiose features immediately set the tone of the house and impressed visitors on their arrival. In prosperous times ever since, miniature versions have been inserted into the houses of the well-to-do.

A grand staircase was usually made of stone for the first flight, but was then reduced to wood for the upper floors. From the 19th century onward, there was an increased use of carpet on stairs, using narrow

strips that showed a small area of polished stone or wood on either side. These were held in place with brass rods that slotted into fixtures at either edge of the carpet at the bottom of the risers. Less important stairs further up the house had narrow drugget carpeting (a coarse, woven fabric), and those leading to the attics were left as bare wood.

In most middle-class houses of the 19th century, the main stairs led straight up from the hall passage to the first (in America, the second) floor, while a second set was placed at the back of the house for servants to use unseen. In small row houses, one staircase sufficed, and this had to make a dog-leg turn for lack of space. A window at the back of the house allowed some light into this rather cramped area.

The Arts and Crafts house of the late 19th century, however, often included a spacious half-landing, where the stair flights, rising through a spacious, double-height hall, turned at right angles to each other. This was also the place for a window, sometimes with stained glass, adding to the quasi-medieval atmosphere. In the hands of the visually imaginative, the half-landing can be a delightful way station. The example shown on page 66 is in Professor Bernard Nevill's West House, an Arts and Crafts property in London's Chelsea. It reveals his passion for antique textiles and furniture, a knowledge he has put to good use in his career as a fabric designer, as head of textile design at the Royal College of Art, and in his own homes. The sense of seclusion is reminiscent of the apartments introduced on the mezzanine or entresol floor (just above the ground floor) in the formal French palaces of the early 18th century. These satisfied a yearning for privacy and comfort, and were small and low-ceilinged but also luxurious. There was no common English equivalent, it seems. For the past 20 years, Nevill has also been restoring his country house in the Gothick ruin of Fonthill Abbey in Wiltshire, begun in 1796 for William Beckford, who started his extravagant project "as an ornamental building which should have the appearance of a convent, be partly in ruins, and yet contain some habitable apartments." Nevill was also an advisor on the restoration of neo-Gothic Eastnor Castle in Herefordshire (built in 1811), where he encouraged the restorers to keep the proportions big and the colors bold, advice that is exemplified by his own London house.

Another house influenced by the Arts and Crafts Movement but built some 50 years later, shown on page 67, includes a half-landing of a different mien. It has been given a crisp, contemporary look by the late Roger Banks-Pye, who designed the house's decoration for David Green, Chairman of Colefax & Fowler. Parts of the house have retained the Arts and Crafts feeling – the unassuming simple lines and the small leaded panes of the casement windows on the landing, for instance, which were typical of the movement, harking back nostalgically to a rather romanticized past and to earlier English vernacular architecture. Other aspects of the movement include an emphasis on handcraft and on the honesty of materials, but Banks-Pye played down this retrospective angle, opting for a comfortable but tailored modern feeling. Though historians urge house owners to conserve the original color of woodwork, it was at Banks-Pye's insistence that the oak paneling and stairs be limed to lighten the hall and stair area. This has imparted an airy quality to the landing and helped to give the house a contemporary atmosphere.

The fancifully painted landing shown above was designed by decorative-paint specialist Jocasta Innes for her own house. She has combined flat painting – big, perfect, red ovals on a cupboard surrounded by books – with a diamond-patterned painted floor, and a textured, painted-on dado.

Contemporary English architects and designers often redesign staircases in existing houses, perhaps giving them open-riser treads, or treads of frosted-glass, which let the light through. In the Hoxton loft belonging to Jason Shulman and Aurora Irvine, a lightweight spiral staircase now leads to a roof garden, and in Seth Stein's Kensington mews house, a sweeping staircase curves around a sitting room space, holding brightly colored contemporary seating and modern sculpture. Both adapt the 1920s and 1930s taste for staircases that could be seen from the principal rooms, in houses conceived as a flow of space.

ABOVE: A half-landing in decorative paint specialist Jocasta Innes's London house shows her skills. The black-and-white, diamond-patterned floor and cupboard painted with red ovals contrast with the yellow ochre walls embellished with a neatly banded dado of faux marble.

LEFT: A fox rug lies on the bed and a 1930s tartan rug over the footboard in Professor Bernard Nevill's dressing room. The bed curtains are heavy silk French damask with an enormous seven-foot repeat, c.1850. They flank an Edwardian mahogany-framed screen of green striped moiré. The cushion on the bed is covered in a Voysey-type Art Nouveau woven cotton. In the foreground is an inlaid Edwardian elbow chair. Family photographs and a Claude Lorraine landscape cram the table. At the far side of the bed is a Regency Honduran mahogany low boy that once belonged to the Earl of Seston. Here, and throughout his house, Nevill uses Edwardian overhead billiards lampshades made of dark green, pleated silk.

BEDROOMS

THE BEDROOM IS ONE ROOM IN THE HOUSE that can be unashamedly feminine. In a family house, it is usually far more the wife's private place than the husband's. Nowadays, women who do not have to check into work at a specific time sometimes even use the bedroom as their office. Privileged ladies of leisure may spend the first hour or so of their morning having breakfast in bed and organizing their diaries and charitable work on the telephone.

The boudoir of the early 18th century was a French invention and was used either as a dressing room, a bedroom, or a sitting room – or a combination of all three. It was a small room where a personal maid laid out her mistress's clothes and arranged her hair, a place where a woman could literally "let down her hair" and "loosen up," in other words, undo the laces of her stays. The boudoir took on risqué connotations because French women invited both men and women in as they dressed. The term was occasionally used in England in order to be *au courant* (it is now only used tongue-in-cheek), but English bedrooms tended to be more staid than those in continental Europe. English women were not in the habit of entertaining guests during the morning "toilette" – the word derives from the 17th-century French term for a white cover on a dressing table.

In town in the 19th century, a Society woman changed her clothes three or four times a day. The morning gown was worn initially, for receiving callers at home, then another outfit for shopping and meeting people outside the house. In the afternoon she wore a tea gown, before dressing formally for dinner. Formal evening wear in some levels of society continued up to and even during the Second World War. The bedroom was where all this changing took place, unless the house was large enough to have a

separate dressing room. Today, a well-appointed bedroom has a dressing room close by, or even two, one for him and one for her. Many have louvered or mirrored doors, special shelves to accommodate hats and bags, drawers to hold hosiery and gloves, and racks for shoes at the bottom. By contrast, textile designer Professor Bernard Nevill's dressing room in his Chelsea Arts and Crafts house (opposite) is a paean to wonderful old fabric, eruditely put together with cherished antique furniture. However, with space in towns at a premium, the luxury of a dressing room remains the preserve of the few.

A free-standing wardrobe or clothes cupboard was essential until built-in clothes cupboards became a standard fixture (initially an American feature, in the late 19th century). The American term "closet" did not catch on in England because, to the squeamish Victorian mind, it sounded a little too much like "water

ABOVE: No book on English rooms would be complete without a chintz-covered bedroom. This one belonged to the late Geoffrey Bennison, a much-admired antiques dealer and purveyor of wonderful chintzes with a vintage, documentary look.

OPPOSITE: Fashion designer Roland Klein's bedroom blends French furniture with an English setting. His London terrace house with its original parquet floor, crown molding, and typical shared garden outside, makes a good setting for a Napoleonic bed, dressed with an antique paisley coverlet. When he found the charming painting of the woman in her Empire dress, he knew she would complement the period frame.

closet," which, incidentally, was always housed in a small room near the bathroom. Victorians could hardly bring themselves to say "bed," and never uttered the word "leg," even when referring to furniture.

Hanging cupboards for clothes have been in use since the Stuart period (1603–1714), but early versions were quite low, and often had bars rather than a solid front, to allow air to circulate. By the end of the 18th century, taller hanging wardrobes became popular, replacing the clothes press or wardrobe with shelves, and in the Victorian period these became massive mahogany cupboards with plate mirrors in the doors. Despite their height, they were not always tall enough to hang women's dresses because of internal drawers at the bottom. Less well-off families were obliged to hang clothes on hooks behind a curtain.

Matching suites of bedroom furniture probably date from the 18th century. As part of a general desire to give rooms an overall coherence, matching fabric would often be used for bed hangings, upholstery, and curtains. With increased mass production in the Victorian era, bedroom suites became popular and might consist not only of a bed, chest of drawers, and dressing table, but also of a wardrobe and bedside tables. A decorative theme would often unite the pieces: fancy inlay or painting on the headboard and footboard of the bed would be repeated on the doors of the wardrobe and on the drawers or some other part of the dressing table. After the First World War, three-piece suites – a bed, wardrobe, and dressing table – became inexpensive and consequently less desirable for the rich and stylish.

The dressing table was first found in mid-17th-century France, and by the turn of the 18th century was used in England by both men and women. Other 18th-century bedroom accessories included leather or wooden wig stands, satinwood dressing cases on narrow legs, and eye-level shaving mirrors with adjustable magnifying lenses. The dressing table has long been an important piece of furniture in town, where dressing well takes on greater significance than it does in the country – although it is now used exclusively by women. Some dressing tables have a froth of *point d'esprit* (or dotted Swiss, an almost sheer cotton) attached to hinged sections that open up to display drawers for make-up and jewelry. The accessories found on a dressing table change with the times. It would once have been covered with pretty embroidered mats, but today the top is more likely to be mirrored or covered in fabric protected by glass. It may still hold 19th-century silver- or tortoiseshell-backed hair and clothes brushes, a fancy pincushion – which in Edwardian days held long, lethal hat pins – bottles of scent with sprays, a ring stand, a tray for hair ornaments, and, popular until the 1960s, a swansdown powder puff in a dish. Up until the early 20th century, there might also have been a home-made "hair tidy" on a wall nearby.

For their accessories, men during the past century have used the top of a bureau, a dressing box on a chest of drawers, or the tray of a silent valet. This last has a stand with a coat hanger, a bar on which to lean shoes, and expanding hangers for ties. Inexpensive examples were frequently used from the mid-20th century. Until clothing became more casual, following the Second World War, most dress shirts had a detachable collar and cuffs requiring cuff links. Men therefore also needed leather stud and collar boxes.

Washbasins were first introduced into bedrooms in the early 18th century. In the following century, many bedrooms had a marble-topped washstand with a basin and ewer that the maid would fill with water

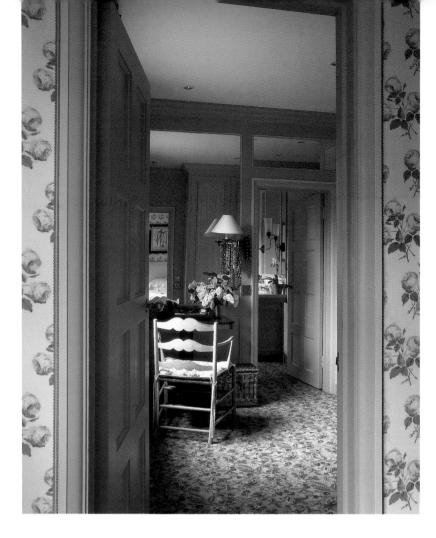

LEFT: Rodney Archer's flair for theatricality – he is a director of drama at the City Institute – reveals itself in this bedroom in his Spitalfields house, where he has introduced a celestial theme. Stars adorn the ceiling and suns decorate the cushions on the bed, although they are balanced by the very English candlewick-style bedspread, plus a sleeping cat. The window has been framed to repeat the flattened arch of the fireplace and mirror above. Pale aqua art pottery on the mantelpiece echoes the color of the bedspread. The walls are stained in shades of green.

for washing, or for the gentleman to use for shaving. This was later replaced in some bedrooms with running water. Not so long ago – up until the 1950s, and perhaps beyond in smaller houses – chamber pots were still in use. In medieval England, as every schoolchild knows, chamber pots, often called "piss pots," were emptied out of the overhanging casement windows right into the street, while the servant yelled "Slops below!" Victorian and Edwardian bedside tables had cupboards to hold chamber pots, but such tables were not in frequent use until the end of the 19th century, after the introduction of electricity.

In houses built before the 1960s when central heating became widespread, every bedroom had a fireplace, even attic bedrooms. The fireplace is still an iconic focus for an English room. Even in Seth Stein's ultra-modern renovation of a mews house in Kensington, he has retained a sleek version in the middle of a wall of bedroom cupboards.

The bedroom at Eltham Palace (see page 64) is the epitome of between-the-Wars chic, when streamlining and sheen were the ultimate in glamor. It was designed by Peter Malacrida (Marchese Malacrida), a friend of the Courtaulds. Entry into Virginia Courtauld's Art Deco-influenced bedroom is through curved, sliding doors. Designed with all the latest Moderne conveniences, the main light source and central heating are concealed in the circular ceiling. A central vacuum system housed in the cellar keeps every room free from dust. Glass-topped brackets set on panels around the room originally held crystal figures that were illuminated from below, and a Classical shrine may once have lodged in the alcove above the bed. The two small pictures are copies of paintings by the Dutch master Jan Bruegel, depicting the elements Air and Water.

ABOVE: The door from David and Judy Green's bedroom leads into a stylish cupboard-lined dressing room with subtle green paintwork chosen by decorator Roger Banks-Pye to complement Colefax & Fowler's classic Bowood design, which was used for both wallpaper and curtains. Beyond the dressing room can be seen the door opening into the bathroom.

LEFT: The six-foot-long enamel bath in Richard Beer's current bathroom was moved from a bathroom that had been on the floor above. He covered the bath sides with plywood and then created a marbleized effect. The Edwardian bath mat may have seen better days but has sentimental value, having belonged to his father's aunt.

Most English people still prefer to sit and soak in a bath rather than take a shower. A portable form of shower was introduced to a very few houses in the 19th century, although the contraption was awkward: hot water was released from a high tank supported by pipes, and then recirculated using a hand pump. Today, English apartments have a separate shower stall, and many baths have a shower gadget attached to the wall (although seldom a shower curtain), but the majority of bathrooms, as shown in these photographs, only have a bath. A warm and relaxing soak is an enjoyable ritual, and the English have developed many forms of scented bath salts, natural essences, and hand-milled soaps to enhance the pleasure.

The first half of the 20th century was dominated by much-vaunted American bathroom plumbing: the hot and cold water mixer, the shower with curtain or glass surround, and the water cistern behind instead of above the loo, which in America, unlike in the majority of English bathrooms, is included in the same room as the tub. In recent decades, the most sophisticated strides in bathroom fixtures have been made by English, Italian, and Japanese designers. Japanese engineering has introduced not only push-button bidet rinses right in the loo, but also a blow dry – and even music. Because of advances in technology and product design, the bathroom, like the kitchen, is one of the most frequently made-over rooms in a house, but there is a distinct and almost inexplicable British resistance to the convenience of taps that mix hot and cold water into one central faucet. As with kitchens, trophy bathroom fittings from English manufacturers such as Czech & Speake and Waterworks are now exported all over the world.

Bathroom equipment has also changed. Costly organic sponges, loofahs, and brushes with natural bristles have been joined by popular electrical devices such as hair dryers, shavers, electric toothpicks,

ABOVE: In this window of Richard Beer's bathroom, papyrus grass and a lace curtain provide privacy. The lace was found at a shop called El Indio in Barcelona. A glass bottle adds color. The statue of a dog made of painted cement was seen by Beer in a shop just outside Vienna one year. Finding it was still there waiting for him the following year, he bought it.

ABOVE: Seth Stein's downstairs loo is housed in a polished cement column in a corridor of his redesigned London mews house. When the door is opened, water automatically pours from a tap into the white marble sink

RIGHT: In actor Peter Eyre's Central London flat, the bath, set into a stone ledge, has been given a copper-effect finish. The surrounding walls have been painted to resemble the stone. On either side are niches with etched glass doors, one holding the loo, the other a shower. Nicholas Haslam helped with the interior design and designed the lighting units.

bath mitts, and weighing scales as essential furnishings of the bathroom. The bathroom linen closet – once the airing cupboard – is no longer filled with plain, white Turkish toweling and the white-on-white finger-tip towels hand-embroidered as part of a young lady's "bottom drawer" in the past. Colored and printed towels came on the scene in the 1950s, and now most of the major fashion designers sell collections of household linen.

In addition to a bathroom – a room with a bath – the powder room or "downstairs loo" has become popular. The word "loo" is a corruption of the French term *lieux à l'angloise*, water closet reputed to have been invented in England. One was certainly made for Queen Anne, and ten were installed at Chatsworth, Derbyshire, seat of the Duke of Devonshire, in the late 17th century. Some balk at the term "powder room" because it sounds like a euphemism from the 1920s, when ladies, who by then frankly admitted to powdering their noses, used it as an excuse to visit the unmentionable water closet. In fact the term "powdering room" dates back to the 18th century, recalling the room where gentlemen powdered their wigs. Powder rooms can

be tiny spaces decorated in a precious style, like the inside of a jewel box. They can also be as starkly modern as Seth Stein's downstairs loo placed in a cylinder of cement (see page 82).

Adjoining, or sometimes part of, a bathroom spa complex, or even next to a study, is the exercise room. Interior designers find that more and more of their clients insist on rooms set aside for health maintenance, body-shaping, and preserving youth and vigor. Taking exercise at home is not new for the Englishman: "bouncing boards" were once used to reduce and strengthen the buttocks, and Indian clubs were popular in the latter half of the 19th century for firming up the arms. The most recent addition to the house or apartment is an aggressively high-tech exercise room. Though not yet the obsession in England that it is in America, the room often includes a media wall to help pass the time on the treadmill.

ABOVE: During the last two decades of the 20th century a new type of room made its way into the town house – the exercise room. Busy executives can ensure they get their necessary physical workout before, after, or even during the working day.

chapter 4

garden rooms

conservatories,
patios, verandahs
& terraces

LEFT: In this dining room conservatory, designer Melissa Wyndham aimed at a Moroccan feel. The chairs, from Ashley Hicks, are set around a skirted table covered with fabric by George Spencer. Overhead roof blinds are pinoleum, and the chandelier was made specially by Gareth Smith. The obelisk is a Mexican light fitting.

ABOVE: A small conservatory room, used for meals, adjoins the kitchen seen on page 51. The mirror behind the large country-style wooden armchair gives the illusion of depth to the limited space. At the other end of the table, a Windsor chair mixes casually with white chairs that can be used in or out of the garden.

ABOVE: This sitting/garden room in David and Judy Green's Hampstead house has shelves for Judy's books on gardening. The simple beige carpet, string-covered coffee table, red-and-white check upholstery, and collection of watering cans create a casual air that makes this room perfect for relaxing and watching television.

AN ESSENTIAL PART OF THE ENGLISH CHARACTER is a love of gardening. The temperate English climate and the lack of dangerous flora and fauna make this island a perfect place for cultivating flowers. Everyone visiting England in the summer is impressed by the lavish displays of well-tended flowers not only in private town gardens but also around lampposts in busy city streets and even in the middle of municipal road junctions. When Londoners move into high-rise apartment blocks, their first complaint is that they have nowhere to garden. They look down on the minuscule row houses below, all with flourishing back gardens, and envy them. Some make do with plants in pots on a tiny terrace, others grow herbs on the window sill or tend window boxes. Though many of the public parks and gardens in England's towns and cities are wonderful – and Queen Mary's Rose Garden in London's Regent's Park is absolutely magical – looking at flowers in city parks is not enough for the true gardener. It is the puttering around in the soil, getting seriously down to earth, that the English crave.

Almost every town house since the Middle Ages has had some sort of a garden, originally in order to accommodate an outside "bog house" (water closet), a wash or cook house, and a skimpy vegetable plot, rather than for privacy. These were at the rear of the house because most medieval houses led directly onto the street. With the advent of city squares, introduced by Inigo Jones (1573–1652), and popularized in the Georgian era, these green spaces allayed the need for front gardens, which only developed toward the end of the 18th and through the 19th century. Though there were notorious slums in London during this later period, where gardens, if they existed, were untended or held shacks for sweat shops, artisans' houses, such as those in Battersea and Kennington, had individual small gardens for a vegetable plot and a few fruit trees. Today, town-house back gardens are sometimes communal areas if the house is divided into apartments, but otherwise they are clearly separated by walls, hedges, or fences.

The back garden of David and Judy Green's Hampstead house is right next to a wildlife sanctuary with a lake and an ever-passing show of water birds. This area of Hampstead was developed in the 1920s, in the wake of Fabianism (a movement that began in 1884 and strove to spread socialist principles by gradual means rather than revolution), and as part of the growing popularity of the garden suburb, which aimed to make tree-lined streets and open spaces available to all. Judy Green's Garden Shop in Hampstead sells furniture and decorative accessories, and such garden-orientated objects feature in her sitting room-cum-garden room at home.

The 17th-century passion for cultivating citrus fruits in an alien climate led to the development of orangeries, such as the vast, glass-windowed Classical building at Versailles, where orange and lemon trees in wooden tubs could survive the winter. In the mid-19th century, public parks, arboretums, and botanical gardens in England added glass houses for growing species such as tomatoes – or even bananas – that would otherwise never have ripened in the intermittent sunshine. By the late 19th century, small greenhouses were being built onto the back of quite modest houses. When they reached larger proportions, they were known as conservatories. In the late Victorian and Edwardian period, these became popular among the affluent as an extra room for meals, and for entertaining against a background

Left: A little rustic garden hut built at the end of a London garden and fitted cunningly between trees, vines and bushes, provides a cool place to take a break from gardening and sit and enjoy a drink.

THE ENGLISH ROOM

of exotic palm trees, bamboo groves, clumps of gigantic grasses, and other sensitive plants. Today, a conservatory with enough room for a table doubles as a dining room, the greenery offering a welcome respite from the noise, brick, and cement of town life. Larger conservatories can be glamorous and glittery for dinner parties at night, with candlelight reflected in the glass walls and roof. Warm, even hot, in the daytime, however, such rooms must incorporate overhead shades. The resplendent conservatory shown on page 89 used to belong to interior designer Nina Campbell. Here, fine matchstick blinds shield the room from daytime sun, while sumptuous blue-and-brown chintz curtains and a chintz-covered screen offer privacy at night. For the winter months, conservatories often have steam-heated pipes that run under the benches carrying seedlings and flowers for cutting, to guard against frost.

Conservatories give people the joy of being surrounded by live, growing plants, and some can even accompany this with the sound of water falling from a fountain. There may only be space for a small tea table and a couple of bamboo chairs, but this too follows precedent, as Edwardian ladies often used to take tea in their conservatories.

France in the 17th century was the fount of everything stylish in Europe, and the exiled English king, Charles II, learned much about its gardens designed in the grand manner – the dramatic avenues, majestic fountains, sumptuous parterres, and sophisticated culture of trees – though unable to afford the excesses of Louis XIV. On a smaller scale, more suited to towns, were the symmetrically designed gardens with small pools, miniature canals and fountains, bordered with intricate topiary, that were introduced into England when William III (1688–1702) and Mary II brought the Dutch garden to Hampton Court and Kensington Palace. The Scotsman John Claudius Loudon focused on creating town gardens for terrace houses. Influential from the early 19th century, Loudon introduced the romance of winding paths, rockeries, rustic arches, and colorful flowers. In the Victorian age, mass production reached the garden and even the humblest could be crammed with garishly colored bedding plants, bought from nurseries or hawkers with barrows.

Gardens attached to town houses are often small, but they can be made to seem larger with careful planning. The elements should include not only trees, bushes, plants, and flowers, but also hard surfaces such as stone, brick or wood, including Classical features such as urns, statues, stone or glass balls, and rockeries, buildings such as garden houses, gazebos, and small eye-catchers, and water, in pools, streams, or fountains. In the 1920s, some garden houses were placed on a wooden turntable arrangement that could be swiveled to catch every ray of the fleeting English sun.

The back garden shown opposite and on page 92 was planned by Christopher Masson, a professional garden designer. The space has been made interesting not only by the planting but also by stone walkways leading to different areas for sitting or for sheltering. There is a simple, rustic garden house. Water is introduced underfoot where tiny stepping stones lead over a diminutive pool to a small terrace with a round table, perfect for outdoor meals. Wooden chairs with concave backs circle the table while, in another part of the garden, chairs with convex backs surround a tree. Partly planted with perennial flowers and bushes,

Above: A metal fire escape that is no longer in use between two loft buildings in Hoxton has become a diminutive garden for growing herbs.

RIGHT: *The red-tiled terrace balcony of Peter Eyre's London flat overlooks not only the Thames but also the London Eye, a huge ferris wheel built by British Airways for the millennium celebrations. Eyre does not even need a clock – he can see the face of Big Ben from the side of his terrace,*

ABOVE: *Though fairly small in scale, this South London garden is astutely organized into different areas, or roofless "rooms." A neat stone terrace becomes the perfect spot for a table set for lunch. The wooden curved-back garden chairs have been chosen to fit around the circular table.*

this well-organized garden also makes good use of movable pots and tubs to give variety and to fill in spaces where necessary. Groups of plants are placed so that the eye is always invited to look further.

The word "terrace," when applied to gardens, suggests a flat, paved-over area close to the house. Terraces in country houses can be extensive, but in city gardens they are more likely to be called by the Spanish name "*patio*," now part of the English garden vocabulary. Sometimes the town garden is so tiny that there is barely room for a stone patio or wooden deck with a table and chairs for eating outside, edged with pots of flowers that can be moved easily. When covered with some sort of roof attached to the house, a patio may be called a "verandah," a Hindi term brought to England at the time of the British Raj. New Englanders call them "porches," screen them against insects and wrap them around the house.

A terrace may be a covered balcony, in which case it might be called by the Italian term "*loggia*." In South Carolina, they are called "piazzas." Actor Peter Eyre's balcony (opposite) is high up in a Central London block of service apartments. Though narrow, it is set about with plants in pots and has the great advantage of looking out onto a magnificent view of the Thames, seen through a screen of mature trees.

A town dwelling may only have space for a window box planted with basil and some primulas. Jason Shulman and Aurora Irvine's top-floor loft in Hoxton has a defunct metal fire escape on which they grow herbs (see page 91). Their roof is reached by a spiral staircase, and in the summertime it is filled with pots of geraniums, petunias, lilies, sweet peas, lavender, and honeysuckle. Even if the space available feels as tiny as a Japanese-style garden in a dish – a fad of the early 20th century – the English are not happy unless they have a garden or a garden room that can be a sheltering spot against the changeable weather.

it hard to resist over-decorating every surface, especially interiors. Ceilings dripped with elaborate plaster stalactites, oak staircases were punctuated with mythical animals, mottoes – for the increasingly literate population – were carved into beams and painted on walls. This Early Renaissance period, variously termed Tudor, Elizabethan, and Jacobean, bore faint resemblance to the re-examined Classical style that so inspired Andrea Palladio (1508–80), until the time of Inigo Jones, England's first important Classical architect and designer. His ascendancy set the stage for the Late Renaissance, the great flowering of English architecture.

Setting the stage was a skill at which Inigo Jones excelled, becoming a celebrated designer of masques. Starting life as a painter, he visited Italy, funded by his patron the 3rd Earl of Pembroke, for whom Jones designed the famous Cube and Double Cube rooms at his country seat, Wilton House, built in the 1630s. Jones was a sophisticated and urbane innovator, designing the seminal Queen's House at Greenwich (1616), commissioned by James I for Anne of Denmark and then re-worked for Charles 1's wife, Henrietta Maria. It was so daringly modern in its time that it was another century, and a new dynasty – the Hanoverians – before the calm, refined English Late Renaissance style Jones pioneered would catch on throughout England. The style came to be known as Georgian.

As the country prospered, from the Tudor period onward, clipper ships brought back all manner of luxury goods to fill England's great country houses. From Genoa came luscious velvet, embossed using a heat process called *gaufrage* (meaning "waffle"), with which the wealthy draped their state beds. Shimmering silk damask – the weave originating in Damascus – and magnificent single velvets and *cord du roi*, originally a regal fabric (its modern derivative is corduroy) came from France. Painted silk taffetas, known as *Pékins*, were brought from China.

A Chinese trade delegation attended Elizabeth I's court, and by the 18th century trade with the Far East had proliferated. Chinese porcelain-making techniques were far in advance of those in Europe at this time. Aristocratic English families commissioned 500-piece sets of china, often bearing armorial arms, and garnitures of Chinese porcelain were arranged on shelves, mantels, and tables. Eventually, first French and German, then English china and pottery works caught up and took on distinct national styles and techniques. Furnishings included Chinese palace chairs, low tables, and carved and lacquered Coromandel screens – named after their port of embarkation in Mandalay. From these imported items the French were the first to adapt their own version, known as "chinoiserie," which was taken up to a lesser extent in England, but notably in Chippendale's Chinese-style chairs.

Despite the Classically inspired architecture of great country houses in the 18th century, these artifacts imported from the East had a noticeable effect on interiors. Many stately homes had a room lined in hand-painted Chinese wallpaper, such as the one at Felbrigg in Norfolk. Even today, there is a fascination with the oriental in the application of Feng Shui, the art of propitious room arrangement, to Western interiors.

Japan traded briefly with England in Queen Anne's reign when Japanese lacquerware was much coveted but, as Japan cut off relations with the rest of the world, trade was not resumed until the late

Victorian and Edwardian eras, when strings of Japanese paper lanterns lit every garden party and "kimono" became part of the English vocabulary. *The Mikado*, though a caricature of Japanese life, was a favorite Gilbert and Sullivan opera. The sophisticated simplicity of traditional Japanese design was not, however, generally appreciated until the mid-20th century in England. Today, the inventive fabrics, fashion, and furniture of Japanese designers influence many interiors.

The English connection with India started with the flourishing trade of the East India Company, established in 1600, which later transferred its power and influence to the British Government. Early imports were only for the wealthy and included such rarities as ivory furniture (examples of which can be seen at the Victoria and Albert Museum in London). From the Regency period, the British promoted Indian cabinet-makers and a whole category of Anglo-Indian furniture developed, its look new and different because of the materials used: padouk wood – the heaviest in the world – and teak, often studded with mother of pearl. Caning was developed in tropical climates because it let the breezes through, and was then introduced to England. These pieces required intensive hand-work, but labor in India was cheaper than in England. For the less affluent, there was bamboo furniture, or, in imitation, faux bamboo. By the end of the 19th century, accessories in the already crowded rooms of the middle classes included Benares brass trays set on folding stands and used as tea tables, and rows of ebony and ivory elephants.

The best preserved of all English rooms are found in great houses, dubbed "The Stately Homes of England." Many are open to the public, although the original families may still live in them. They are known as "Grade I" buildings, and like all buildings in Britain of any age and architectural interest, are graded according to their importance. Their styles range from castle strongholds through Tudor, Baroque, neo-Classical, Greek Revival, Italianate, and Victorian Gothic Revival. The rooms reflect the history and interests of the family and provide valuable evidence of changes to English style.

In the 18th century, land immediately surrounding great neo-Classical houses became fashionably park-like, replacing the earlier, formal parterre or topiary gardens. Romantic ruins known as "follies" – bridges, fountains, temples, and buildings that were sometimes used as small banqueting houses – were strategically placed in the landscape as eye-catchers. Some follies were even large enough to live in.

The Gothick literary movement was the inspiration for The Castle, a lived-in eye-catcher on the Sledmere estate. Gothick taste embraced the concept of "picturesque" scenery, which emphasized Nature in all its primal power and the emotive quality of craggy cliffs, moss-laden trees, ruined "horrid" castles, and desecrated abbeys. By the beginning of the 19th century, Gothick style had become fully fledged as the Romantic movement, a reaction against the logic of the neo-Classical Enlightenment and focusing on the role of emotion and feeling as opposed to reason, highlighting the importance of "sensibility," a fashionable word of the era.

Grand stately homes are few in number compared to the many charming manor houses that distinguish the English countryside. Some of these manor houses are early enough to have a moat – such as Ightham Mote in Kent. Most, however, were built when fortifications were no longer needed because the country had reached a more settled way of life. The area closest to a manor house often includes beautiful gardens, a brick-walled kitchen garden, a greensward with sheltering trees, plus orchards, a carriage house and stables, and many also have acreage used for farming and hunting.

The rectory, parsonage, or vicarage is a more humble type of house that was once used by a clergyman and his family and can be found in most country villages. Smaller than a manor, they were the home of many living on a modest though respectable income, such as the writer Jane Austen and her family. The most delightful examples are Regency Gothick in style. There is often a greenhouse attached to the back of the house, and a lawn for croquet or tennis. Vicarage gardens are frequently the most interesting in the village because Gentlemen of the Cloth tended to be knowledgeable about botany and had extensive libraries with (now much-collected) books on horticulture. Today, abandoned and deconsecrated nonconformist chapels are sometimes made over into interesting small houses.

The early part of the 19th century produced particularly appealing domestic interiors. Influenced by expeditions made during the Napoleonic Wars, architecture, furniture, and even clothing reflected Ancient Greek, Roman, and even prettified Egyptian influences, as well as the picturesque Gothick style. Sitting rooms in more modest houses were particularly winsome. Simple stripes, flower-sprigged cottons, dimity, mousseline, and muslin were popular. Painted Regency furniture was popular for much of the 20th century because of its unassuming simplicity, and is still much sought after. Slipcovers tied at the back with bows, needlepoint carpets, modestly patterned wallpapers with applied borders, lacquered fire screens, sewing boxes on stands, all displayed a new delicacy that would be lost in the florid confections popular later in the 19th century. Almost all these furnishings are easy to live with and are still well-liked.

Most English villages have a main street that is an old, narrow thoroughfare with houses on both sides, or surrounding a communal village green that may be used for fairs or cricket matches. Often there is a stream or a duck pond. Village houses may be placed closely together with walled gardens at the back. The houses sometimes touch, as do those on The Street in Woolpit, Suffolk, where a row of houses built in the Tudor period was updated with fashionable Georgian fronts two centuries later, thus enlarging the small-paned leaded window apertures into larger sash windows. Village houses might be discreetly tucked behind hedges with small front gardens and larger ones at the back. The scale of village houses is modest – two, or at most three, floors – some with low, beamed ceilings. The village house is not as self-consciously cute as a cottage even though the upstairs bedrooms might be tucked under the eaves.

The interior decoration of village houses nowadays comes in a range of styles from antique to modern, using fabrics from plain linen to floral chintz, but anything pretentiously ornate or expensive-looking is considered inappropriate. Comfort, practicality, family bits and pieces, plenty of books and good light to read by, a place to dine for weekend guests, and an engrossing garden are the chief aims of a country village house.

The architect Edwin Lutyens (1869–1944) was responsible for the design of many early 20th-century country houses, as well as making a name for himself with public buildings as far afield as New Delhi. His

first passion, however, was for Surrey's village houses, cottages, and farm buildings, and, inspired by Norman Shaw, Philip Webb and the Arts and Crafts movement, he designed houses in that county using local materials and techniques such as half timbering and tile-hung roofs. His later fame rested to a greater extent on his revival of interest in Queen Anne and Georgian architecture, albeit with his own distinctive romantic notions and picturesque silhouettes. He formed a working partnership with garden designer Gertrude Jekyll (1843–1932), a woman of many talents including embroidery and photography, who eschewed the formal flower beds so beloved by Victorians in favor of more natural arrangements of herbaceous borders and allowing the garden to become an "outdoor room" – an extension of the house.

Until the 20th century, farmhouses were built solely for the farmer and his family. The house, with the exception perhaps of a seldom-used "front room" – a sitting room or parlor – was used simply as working or sleeping space. Whether built of stone or brick, farmhouses were rough, practical rather than pretty, and anything but comfortable. Halls and kitchens had stone-flagged floors that would be icy cold in winter. As farmers clung to their family farmsteads into the 1950s, these floors were covered over with usually hideous linoleum in an attempt at warmth, easy maintenance, and modernity.

A great many farm areas have now become bedroom communities for people who drive to work in not-so-nearby towns. The linoleum has been ripped up to show the patina of well-worn flagstones but central heating, or that favorite of country folk, the Aga, is installed to give warmth. The rough and ready look of the farmhouse has been preserved, but a softening coziness superimposed, even though some of these buildings are large and rambling. Now that there are fewer working farmers, their deserted houses have been idealized. Today's owners roam antique shops for dairy basins, vintage kitchen gadgets, rag rugs, milking stools, oak chests, farm implements, and Windsor chairs to recreate the authentic farmhouse look.

Cottages did not become sought-after as an aesthetic type of dwelling until the early 19th century, spurred on by the influence of the Lakeland poets. Prior to this, they had been considered hovels. Now romanticized, cottages are defined mainly by their scaled-down, land-hugging size, tiny windows, and simple arrangement of rooms, which are kept to a minimum. Old English cottages are extraordinarily varied because they had to be built of local materials. Clay, mud, turf, and wychert – a rare clay-like substance – were all used, but the longest lasting of these was cob, a form of mud strengthened with various ingredients such as lime and chopped reed. Old cob cottages are still found in Devon and Somerset. Oak was a favored building wood until the forests were depleted, but half-timbering is still seen in the counties bordering or close to Wales, such as Cheshire, Shropshire, and Worcestershire, because the Welsh forests were cut down later than those in England. Flint and pebble cottages can be found in Norfolk, limestone cottages in the Cotswolds, millstone grit cottages in Derbyshire, tile-hung fronted cottages in Sussex, slate fishermen's cottages leading down to the sea in Cornwall, plus many colour variations of brick all over the country, depending on the kiln, clay, and fuel of the area. If a cottage also happens to have a thatched roof it wins the highest points for picturesqueness, especially because there are only 50,000 thatched cottages left in England.

Inside a cottage we may expect to find a homey living room with a kettle on the hearth, gingham curtains, afghans on the armchair, and a teapot in a hand-knitted cozy on a table with a hand-embroidered tablecloth. That is almost a stereotype now. In reality, there may be masses of books, efficient plumbing in a bedroom or a passage converted into a bathroom, plus the latest in computer technology.

The English have always been inordinately fond of animals, treating them, one suspects, with an affection sometimes greater than that for their own children. From the royal family on down, the breeding of horses and dogs has been an important pursuit, whether for hunting, racing, or, in the past, for farm work. Stables were always important adjuncts to great houses, such as the Classical 18th-century stable wings at Houghton Hall in Norfolk and the tack room at Calke Abbey in Derbyshire. Stables of a simpler nature were essential to farms, however. As with mews cottages today, farm stables are frequently renovated into rentable, self-contained flats. Some retain the basic, rustic look, leaving the inner walls unfinished, the ceiling beams untouched, and many of the original details in place – such as a cartouche of farm implements decoratively fixed to the wall. Alternatively, barns can be given a sophisticated overhaul, with plastered walls, upholstered furniture, and atypical antiques, or used as open-plan housing, or as superb places for entertaining.

Of all the country pursuits, gardening probably ranks the highest. Great houses employ professional gardeners who test botanical species, though the prettiest sight can be a naive cottage garden that mixes marigolds, cabbages, and hollyhocks in glorious profusion. The English love to potter in garden and greenhouse – and are very good at it. In the 19th century, vast glass houses were constructed, from Decimus Burton's Palm House at Kew in 1844 to Sir Joseph Paxton's "Hothouses for the Million" in 1860. Many self-respecting middle-class houses were considered incomplete without a conservatory that could be used as an extra room for meals. Large, domed conservatories and glassed-in passages were added to stately homes and manors. Even a working-class family might have had a small lean-to greenhouse for starting plants before bedding them out in neat rows in the front garden. The English create cutting gardens to avoid having to take flowers from their meticulously planned herbaceous borders, growing extra edging plants to fill in spaces in case some fail. They arrange cut flowers with insouciant skill, sceptical of anything that looks contrived. Some houses have flower-arranging rooms with deep sinks, high taps and a variety of vases ranged on shelves.

Commemorating the turn of the millennium, a number of garden-proud people built new follies, such as a towering obelisk, a Classical pool house, a wood henge (square pillars supporting horizontal beams – as in Stonehenge), stone arches, small banqueting houses, round towers, all commandeering age-old architectural forms. It is, however, impossible to ignore the fact that straddling town and country today is a growing blend of both. Suburban properties range from small bungalows to large, free-standing houses. The difference between town, suburbia, and country inevitably continues to blur as towns spread, villages prosper, and cars proliferate. It is perhaps comforting to know that almost any house has a chance of being considered amusing, then charming, and finally desirable it if survives at least half a century.

downstairs

ABOVE: Contrasting with a red hallway, glass-paned doors lead the eye through the conservatory and its calming, sun-touched foliage and into a courtyard beyond.

entrance *halls*, sitting *rooms*, libraries & studies

LEFT: The sitting room in interior decorator and antiques dealer Charles Beresford Clark's country house boasts a late 18th-century restored cupboard, possibly designed by Soane, and a chimney piece put in by Clark. The architectural print is of the Admiralty archways in Whitehall by Adam. A door leads to the conservatory added on by Clark.

ENTRANCE HALLS

IN CONTINENTAL EUROPE GREAT HOUSES are often palaces within a town, but in England the great country house is a center of power and it is the produce of the land around it that has traditionally been its support. The long drive up to a great house gives the viewer an idea of the vast acreage, which may be roamed by deer. It provides a distant or sudden, staggering view of the house itself, while cattle and sheep nibble grass beneath sheltering trees. The first impression that cultivated parkland gives is an appropriate build-up to the "home office."

The entrance to a Norman or Gothic castle was reached after crossing a moat with a menacing drawbridge, which could be pulled up if you were not welcome. Once inside the intimidating portals, studded with spiked hinges, bars, and bosses, the great hall was itself imposing in size.

The great 18th-century English houses, inspired by Palladio and built for Whig politicians, were designed to impress the viewer not with fierceness but with quality, discernment, and a magnificent display of wealth. The entrance lobby at Houghton Hall (1722–31) in Norfolk, known as the Stone Hall and perhaps the most beautiful room in England, is a 40-foot (12-meter) cube with a stucco ceiling and a frieze of cherubs by the Venetian stuccoist Giuseppe Artari, stone walls, a balcony with balusters, and an elaborate chimney piece sculpted by John Michael Rysbrack, as well as a black-and-white marble floor and robust benches designed by William Kent.

Holkham Hall (1735–62), also in Norfolk, and Kedleston Hall (1759–65) in Derbyshire have equally imposing marble entrance halls. Marble was the flooring of choice for these grand houses, with black-and-white marble being imported from Italy and other types being drawn from England's mineral-rich counties. Derbyshire could supply not only varieties of colored marble but also the more costly Blue John, which was used for decorative vases and statues.

Front halls on a modest scale that date back to the time of the Stuarts (1603–1714) can be found in manor houses such as Aubourn Hall (remodeled before 1628) in Lincolnshire and Eyam Hall in Derbyshire. In the latter (see page 111), the main hall is entered directly from the front door and has now become a busy, all-purpose family drawing room. Since 1992 the Wright family – who have lived in the house since it was built in 1671 – have opened certain rooms of historic interest to the public. Because of wear to the gracefully shaped, diamond-patterned flagstones in the hall, they have had to be partially covered with a carpet. In 1671 this style of flagstone would have indicated that this was an affluent household, for such a remote area, where no expense was spared. The ceiling beams were once plastered, hence the notched finish to help anchor the plaster in place. The fireplace surround and mantelshelf are 18th century – an earlier, 17th-century surround was discovered underneath in 1991 but was too damaged to reclaim. Family swords hang above the fireplace while, flanking it, are two rare "bacon settles," mentioned in a 1694 inventory of the house and so called because flitches of bacon used to be hung in the tall cupboards.

The house was built on the site of a previous yeoman house on the main street of Eyam, a place famous as the "Plague Village." It was here that the plague traveling north from London in 1665 was stopped owing to the heroism of the villagers, who collectively isolated themselves, knowing they were going to die, to

OPPOSITE: Wilton House in Wiltshire, seat of the Earls of Pembroke and Montgomery, was designed in the newest Palladian style by Inigo Jones in the 17th century. More than a century later, a Gothic cloister-like arcade was inserted into the inner courtyard by the architect James Wyatt, who made various other Gothic-inspired additions to the house.

ABOVE: A devastating fire, caused by a smoldering spark from a worker's blowtorch in 1990, made it necessary to reconstruct most of the interior of the late Jacobean Harrington Hall. The original diamond-shaped flagstones in this entrance hall, though scorched, survived. The central table, and the phoenix on the cabinet which was carved by a local artisan, were both made from wood rescued from the blaze.

RIGHT: The entrance hall at Calke Abbey, Derbyshire, was remodelled around 1841 by combining two rooms and rebuilding a stone "back" staircase. A low-ceilinged room for its size, this dowdy but very English hall is decorated with heads of cattle bred on the estate. Animals and sport were dear to the somewhat eccentric Jenney family, who re-established the older family name, Harpur-Crewe, before Calke became a National Trust property. Never an abbey — that part of the name was added in 1808 when Gothic abbeys were considered romantic — Calke was built in about 1115 as a religious retreat for Augustinian priests who sought an austere, reclusive life. The bulk of the present neo-Classical house was built between 1702–4.

prevent further contamination. Eyam Hall, made of a local stone known as millstone grit, was built by Thomas Wright for his son John to help him join the gentry, and at Eyam there was, presumably, not much competition. The house has a rough, romantic charm typical of this part of the county and its hall has remained remarkably intact for almost 400 years.

By contrast, the entrance hall at Harrington Hall in Lincolnshire (see page 106) has been reconstructed to be identical to the original. Shortly after the present owners bought this late Jacobean manor house and while they were restoring it prior to moving in, an accidental fire destroyed most of the interiors. Though all the working rules had been obeyed – such as stopping the use of blowtorches at least half an hour before the end of the working day – a cinder had lodged behind some paneling, smoldered, and burst into flames in the middle of the night. Every scrap of building material that could be salvaged was reused, but most of the interior architectural detail had to be reconstructed. Interior designer Christopher Nevile, who started out as a painter, and Justin Meath Baker, who had trained as a landscape architect, formed a partnership in 1988 and together they were responsible for the splendid new interiors at Harrington Hall in the 1990s. Christopher Nevile lived nearby at Aubourn Hall, and it was he who eventually worked most closely with the family.

The hall at Calke Abbey in Derbyshire (see page 107) reflects the unusually reclusive temperament and tastes of the Harpur-Crewe family, who lived there until the 1980s, when the house and estate became the property of the National Trust. The original 12th-century structure was built as a religious retreat for Augustinian monks. However, it was never an abbey – the title was added out of nostalgia in the early 19th century. The bulk of the house was built in about 1702 by the Harpurs (later called Harpur-Crewe), a gentry family who rose to wealth – at one point they were among the richest families in England – and who were the owners of several estates.

Some members of the family were as withdrawn as the early monks. One, who lived at the end of the 18th century, was so reclusive that he was dubbed the "isolated Baronet." The last two baronets, Sir John and Sir Vauncey, though taking little pleasure in human society, had no trouble with animals, dead or alive. They spent most of their time with a gun on the estate. Their Longhorn cattle, Portland sheep, prize oxen, and deer, of which there were two herds, are commemorated in the entrance hall, a rather unprepossessing low-roofed room that is almost underground. It gives the impression that your company is not sought. By 1840, the rest of the house contained 200 cases of stuffed birds, quadrupeds, and fish, plus minerals, fossils, and butterflies. By 1924, the number of glass cases had climbed to several thousand. They reached so high that they almost covered the ancestral portraits in the reception rooms and created an obstacle course through the house. The last of the family to live at Calke Abbey, the Jenneys – who reverted to a hyphenated version of the family name, Harpur-Crewe, when the eldest son, Charles, served as High Sheriff in 1961 – kept the house untouched, as though in a time warp. It is faded and dowdy, but very English, and it is these qualities that now make the house so fascinating for visitors.

OPPOSITE: In the dining room of interior decorator Christopher Gibbs's country house, an 1848 statue of Sappho by William Theed the Younger is reflected in an arched, mirrored niche. Reflected also is an open door leading to the hall. A companion statue of Narcissus was in the same room (see page 149), but both statues have now been auctioned.

Hallways in more humble country houses, after 1800, whether parsonages, farmhouses or cottages, reflected the size of the property. Large, flourishing farmhouses were set in walled courtyards, where the workaday entrance to the house would have been the back door, which led to a flagstoned kitchen or laundry. The front door, which was used only by special visitors, might have opened onto a hall, but often led straight into the front parlor. Cottages lacked halls altogether: the door opened directly onto the "front room," an all-purpose space used for eating, sitting, cooking at the fireplace, and bathing in front of it in a portable bathtub.

With the resurgence of interest in vernacular architecture during the Arts and Crafts period, a baronial version of the town house's lounge hall became popular from the mid-19th century to the 1930s, but it was now called the "living hall." Country houses were built with medieval-style details and minstrels' galleries, but with the additional comforts of modern living, such as gas or electric light, although this did not always obscure the fact that their halls, often larger than those in town, were drafty thoroughfares for people passing from one part of the house to another. Grander living halls had hammer-beam ceilings, original or reproduction tapestries, and even a knight in armor.

In the Tudor period, important houses included a long gallery, which was used for walking during days of inclement weather, and for the display of family portraits and other works of art. Knole in Kent (begun in 1456 and enlarged and embellished in 1603) is one of England's great treasure houses, with several long galleries. The Brown Gallery houses an unrivalled collection of Jacobean furniture, while another gallery contains portraits and copies of Raphael cartoons. Hardwick Hall (finished *c.*1597) in Derbyshire has the

longest gallery, at 166 feet (51 meters). Haddon Hall, also in Derbyshire, was originally held by William the Conqueror's bastard son, Peveril of the Peak, in the 12th century, but took its present form in the 14th century. It has an especially lovely long gallery, with carved paneled walls, a white ornamental-plaster ceiling, and lead-paned window, through which daylight streams.

In the 18th century, grand marble and stone passages were introduced into Georgian houses by the supremely wealthy as an alternative to sculpture rooms, for the display of the Classical statues and busts that had been brought back to England from the Grand Tour. At Castle Howard in Yorkshire (started in 1699 by playwright-architect John Vanbrugh, with Nicholas Hawksmoor), the Antique Passage is an arched corridor lined with Classical busts set on gilded plinths designed by William Kent.

ABOVE: The front hall at Eyam Hall in Derbyshire, built in 1671, is also a much-used drawing room. The large group portrait shows the Kniveton Family. The young girl on the left, Elizabeth, married John Wright, for whom Eyam Hall was built. Members of the Wright family have lived in the house ever since.

RIGHT: The Tapestry Room at Eyam Hall is a charming upstairs parlour. The walls are covered from floor to ceiling with tapestry in a combination of periods and styles, even on the thick, stone window insets. Two 17th-century samplers and some 1633 stumpwork have been used as patches. The chair dates from the George I period.

LEFT: Halls and hall passages may stand in for the ever-useful mud or boot room. Lined with wellingtons, umbrellas, and mackintoshes, the room takes the brunt of dirt brought in from a walk in the woods. This passage is also a place of refuge for the family's dogs.

Wilton House in Wiltshire – another contender for the most beautiful house in England – was originally an abbey, given to the 1st Earl of Pembroke in 1542 after the Dissolution of the Monasteries, then remodeled "in the Italian style" for the 4th Earl of Pembroke in the 1630s with advice from Inigo Jones, who had by then become King Charles I's Surveyor-General of Works. Jones was responsible for the restrained Classical exterior and spectacularly flamboyant gold and white interiors of the famous Single and Double Cube rooms. For the 11th Earl of Pembroke, architect James Wyatt added wide neo-Gothic cloister-like corridors around the turn of the 19th century, used both to display the family's collection of sculpture and to aid the flow of traffic within the house (see page 105). This passage got a new fillip when, in the 1950s, John Fowler suggested glazing the walls canteloupe orange to relieve Wyatt's rather dreary grey.

On a less extravagant scale, Ebberston Hall in Yorkshire, built in 1718, is a miniature villa, or "small rustick edifice" as it was described by its architect, Colen Campbell, who had also drawn up the original plans for Houghton Hall. Campbell was inspired by Inigo Jones's Queen's House at Greenwich, built in the first half of the 17th century, and produced at Ebberston one of the most original houses of its date in England. The builder was William Thompson, bachelor M.P. for the nearby seaport of Scarborough and Warden of the Royal Mint. The house is more a hunting lodge than a stately home but its architecture, as can be seen in the passage shown on page 110, has a monumental quality combined with a delightful air of fading refinement. The flagstones are deliberately distinguished from those of manor houses and farmhouses by being arranged as diamonds, considered more elegant than those placed as squares.

COMPARED TO LIFE IN THE CITY, where the ambitious are frequently on the move, country folk tend to stay in one place. In town, people may change domiciles several times a decade, but a country family often lives in the same place for several generations, and many have lived in the same house for centuries. Possessions accumulate in the country, documenting the family's history and pursuits. The country house reflects times past and seldom needs to be up-to-date in the city sense – in fact there is a certain pride in not being fashionable. If a professional decorator assists with a refurbishment, the house will no doubt look far more attractive to that particular generation, but it also runs the risk of appearing to try too hard.

Foreigners still view the English as traditionalists with a rigid class system, reflected in the usual hierarchy of aristocrats in the stately home, gentry in the manor house, professionals in the vicarage, the

SITTING
ROOMS

RIGHT: Built in the 1750s in Northamptonshire, the Menagerie had fallen into a state of disrepair when house historian Gervase Jackson-Stops made it his domicile. He asked sculptor Christopher Hobbs to repair the freehand decoration that was missing from the beautiful rococo plasterwork for which the Menagerie is famous; the circular plaques depict the signs of the zodiac, while above each urn are trophies of arms for four continents. These outsize plaster urns were made by Hobbs to fit the wall niches. All the upholstery fabrics are different but blend in a seemingly uncontrived mix. The skirted table in the foreground has a glass top to protect the fabric; beside it is a volume of Burke's Peerage. Through the open doorway can be seen a painting in the study (see page 133).

ABOVE: Called the Great Drawing Room, this imposing, heavily gilded room at Badminton House, Gloucestershire, is shown here by daylight. It can come alive at night as a music room and, with the carpet rolled back and the sconces lit, it becomes a ballroom. At the far end there are two pianos, one covered with family photographs.

farmer in the farmhouse, and God (an Englishman, of course) in his heaven. This falls far short of the present-day truth. Some of the great houses have been taken over by organizations such as the National Trust and English Heritage, although often the family who have lived there for generations stay in part of the house, while the most impressive and formal rooms are open to the public. Centuries-old decaying manors change hands and may be bought and restored by those who have done well more recently. Country vicarages have long since become too expensive for the average member of the clergy to maintain, and we continually hear about the plight of the farmer who can no longer sustain the living or the farmhouse. The way in which these houses are decorated inside by newcomers to the country often reflects a longing to maintain a mythical status quo. Nowhere is this more apparent than in the sitting room of a country house.

Early "withdrawing" rooms in the cold, damp, stone-walled castles of England were hung with tapestries to provide decoration and a sense of warmth. Rooms in Hardwick Hall, which dates from the Tudor period, are decorated with Brussels tapestries, which were very expensive at the time and enabled the owner, Bess of Hardwick, to display her wealth. Subjects depicted on tapestries at this date included episodes from Classical mythology, biblical and historical scenes, and the decorative presentation of aspects of everyday life. At Hampton Court, during the reign of Henry VIII (1509–47), tapestries were changed every week. Though tapestries can be appreciated by specialists, they now tend to have a deadening effect on a room because their original, brilliant colors have faded over time. At Eyam Hall, however, the walls of a small Jacobean upstairs parlor (see page 113) are covered in a haphazard patchwork

LEFT: Decorator Robert Kime installed an 18th-century stone fireplace into his sitting room and placed above it, dominating the room, a fascinating Elizabethan portrait. Dated 1605, it bears a Latin inscription which translates as: "Why should the husband have believed the wife?" Full of Shakespearean-style puns and hidden references, such as "the half sun, bar sinister, empty scabbard, lack of coat of arms and pickax," the painting subtly reveals itself to be the portrait of a wife's bastard son. In the foreground, behind the sofa, is an Italian Renaissance cassone from Bologna. The rock crystal chandelier is French and 18th-century. In the far corner is an 11-foot (3.3-meter) Chinese lacquer screen; the 18th-century mirror was designed by James Gibbs.

of tapestries that have been beautifully restored. One wall is made up of 11 pieces of Flemish tapestry. At the right-hand corner by the window is a particularly fine 15th-century Flemish example, worked in silk and wool, that depicts figures eating strawberries and fruits from a platter. The tapestries were originally hung to keep out drafts rather than for decoration. They were restored in the 1990s, when new battens were put in place and Velcro supports added, so that the tapestries could hang evenly and be taken down without further damage. At the same time, the windows were fitted with ultra-violet filters to lessen deterioration caused by light. This jigsaw of scraps of antique tapestry gives the room a unique charm.

In a great house, a formal drawing room is large, luxurious, and can be intimidating. The room may be grand and astonishingly beautiful, such as the Single Cube Room at Wilton House, built in the 1630s, with its Kent and Chippendale furniture, gilding, red velvet, and painted pine. It is a room to admire, analyze, and wonder at, but the furnishings are far too precious to be used regularly. Large formal drawing rooms can take on a number of uses. The famous Double Cube Room at Wilton House has been used variously as a dining room, a ballroom, and a drawing room. The Great Drawing Room at Badminton House in Gloucestershire (see page 114), built in the 1740s, makes good use of its imposing proportions and a wealth of gilding to function as a ballroom.

Less grandiose than the drawing room, but more personal, is the sitting room. The superb architectural structure of the great central room in The Menagerie, Northamptonshire (see page 115), is softened by the seemingly artless but in fact highly sophisticated manner of its decoration. The Menagerie was built for Lord Halifax as a folly in the 1750s by the astronomer, architect, and garden designer Thomas Wright,

ABOVE: At Burghley House, the sitting room, shown here, is a place to sit, a library, and a place to have meals. Bookshelves with Classical details are filled with leather-bound books. These are echoed by the brown striped wallpaper, and the room is lightened by the plaster ceiling. The table is set for afternoon tea.

dubbed "the Wizard of Durham." (Follies are eye-catching idiosyncratic buildings, which were sometimes built in landscaped parks to highlight a view. Wright was also responsible for various "eye-catchers" at Badminton House.) The Menagerie was given its title because Lord Halifax's collection of exotic animals roamed the surrounding gardens. The building has a large, single-cube, central room with a coved ceiling, which opens into rectangular alcoves with little square lobbies on either side. The house is famous for its beautiful 18th-century plasterwork depicting signs of the zodiac, which was restored by sculptor Christopher Hobbs when the late Gervase Jackson-Stops, a house historian, transformed the property from its former dilapidated state and made it his home. During the same period a local carver, Lenny Goff, made new consoles (seen on the right of the sitting room), aptly depicting Noah and a parade

of animals. Decorator Melissa Wyndham also helped to restore the fabric and upholstery, including an 18th-century family counterpane embroidered with animals (shown in the foreground covering a table).

London antiques dealer and interior decorator Charles Beresford Clark found his country house near the south coast of England in the 1980s. As he describes it, it was a mundane, four-square workman's house with rather pinched proportions. It had been built in 1912 as one of several houses owned by farmers who mined the local chalk pits to produce lime used to make mortar for the building trade and for fertilizer. Clark set about the daunting task of giving the house his magic touch. Having lived previously in Georgian houses with more generous dimensions, moving into the rather meaner proportions of the Edwardian era was a challenge. He picked a year, 1845, and gradually assembled furniture and added subtle touches to the exterior of the house, such as arched window frames and a porch, that were compatible with the period but did not stick to it too slavishly. To the sitting room (see page 102) he added a conservatory, looking out onto a topiary garden. In 1996, he built on a large, modern kitchen.

When asked what sums up an English room, most people immediately think of a country sitting room with a classic floral chintz covering the sofa and armchairs – a look that has changed relatively little since the Regency period. Printed cotton, using fast colours, was first imported in quantity from India in the 18th century and has risen and fallen in popularity ever since. It is particularly valued for its light, informal effect, in contrast to velvet or heavy, complex weaves. English loose covers in these rooms have always had a somewhat unfitted demeanor, as if, as Keith Irvine says, "Nanny had cut them on the kitchen table with a knife and fork and run them up in her spare time." Shaped loose covers came into use as early as

ABOVE: The curtains in this sitting/billiards room are of a large-scale, exotic floral fabric, while on the armchair is a smaller scale stripe, and the cushions have a tiny print. Yet all the patterns are related by color. Porcelain is displayed in the built-in cupboard with glass panes divided by curved astragals. Family photographs are displayed in silver frames.

RIGHT: The original layout of this cricket pavilion, restored by architect Alfred Munkenbeck, was a one-story structure with changing rooms at one end, a kitchen at the other and the club room in between. The upstairs floor was added in the restoration. The room has a weekend casualness, with simple unlined curtains and wicker and rattan furniture with white canvas upholstery. The table in the eating area was designed by Munkenbeck. It works on a metal frame like an ironing board and can be raised as a dining table or lowered to coffee-table height. The floor, partially sanded, is of thick pine, with an interesting, pock-marked texture resulting from the tread of countless feet in spiked cricket boots.

LEFT: In this seaside sitting room on the Norfolk coast, designed by Chris Cowper, French windows lead out to timber-slatted balconies with diagonal rails. Sofas have been covered in plain and striped light-colored fabrics so as not to fade in the reflected light. Sheer curtains that catch the breeze soften the windows. In the evening, airy Japanese lanterns veil electric lights.

1685, probably originating in the simple sheets thrown over furniture to protect more expensive fabric upholstery. In more recent years, slipcovers have often been bought ready made in "one size fits all" styles that make a practical feature of their almost too loose fit. The country-house sitting room also has plenty of needlepoint cushions, preferably Victorian, stuffed with down and never all matching. Staffordshire dogs, which until the 1960s were inexpensive decorative figures, flank fireplaces. Collections of porcelain and pottery – such as Lowestoft, blue-and-white Canton, and Blind Earl (which has raised details, rather like braille) – are arranged on shelves or hang, apparently, from vertical ribbons. Polished wood floors show beneath old Axminster, oriental, or Wilton carpets: the aim is to present layers of family history. (Broadloom carpeting, which introduced the possibility of fitted, wall-to-wall carpets, was only introduced

in the late 19th century.) Curtains with pelmets puddle slightly on the floor; these are lined, and interlined with flannel, using the best English methods. A round side table with a floor-length table skirt holds family photographs in silver frames. Lamp bases are made from Chinese jars or perhaps employ decalcomania — a pastime of Victorian ladies that involved sticking colored paper scraps inside jars and bottles. Lamp shades are cream-colored silk or pricked card. There is the smell of good furniture wax and fresh flowers.

A room with this "country house" feel is shown on page 118, but this is in fact within a Methodist chapel no longer used for worship. The building has the desirable virtues of the country parsonage: it is on an attractive village street, the chapel sanctuary is the perfect size for a large drawing room, and the room has arched, gothic windows, which are today viewed as charming, not churchy.

ABOVE: *A corner of the sitting room at Chevithorne Barton is ready for afternoon tea. The curtains and two of the cushions are covered in a blue-and-white patterned cotton based on an 1810 batik made famous in the 1950s by poet and muse Louise de Vilmorin, who decorated her entire drawing room at Verrières in it. Chairs have striped seat pads.*

Some sitting rooms are also games rooms. In the 19th century, a grand house would have had a separate billiards room, possibly next to the library, both of them part of the male preserve. At Chevithorne Barton in Devon (see page 119), a large billiards table takes up much of the space, but nowadays such rooms are shared by both sexes. Other sitting rooms are used, as they would have been in the past, as places for light meals. With the increasing popularity of tea in England, bone china, silver accessories, and tea tables, needed to set up a suitable "at home," were produced in large quantities in the latter half of the 18th century. These were used especially by ladies for entertaining friends in the afternoon during the 19th century and up to the Second World War, when more women became wage-earners. A charming blue-and-white sitting room at Chevithorne Barton is shown on page 122, ready for afternoon tea. At Burghley House in Cambridgeshire (see page 117), a more formal tea is laid in a library sitting room. (There seems to be a growing trend to describe such meals as "high tea," perhaps in an attempt to sound grand. High tea was, in fact, the name given to the working-man's supper, especially in country areas, up to and possibly after the Second World War. It was accompanied by a pot of tea and took place between five and six o'clock in the evening.) In smaller houses today, the tea trolley – a very English piece of furniture – may be wheeled in from the kitchen, or sandwiches and scones served from a three-tiered cake stand.

From the 18th century, many aristocratic families with a country seat would spend a certain amount of time "in Town," meaning in London. This habit developed into "The Season," which centered around June. By contrast, in the 19th century, middle-class families living in towns began to have "summer holidays"– a vacation in August when they moved to the country or rented a seaside villa. By the end of the 20th century, it had become fashionable to have a weekend house to escape the busy city life on a more regular basis. The main sitting room (see page 120) in the weekend seaside retreat of architect Chris Cowper, his wife Julia, a textile designer, and their two sons, is situated on an upper floor, partly in case of floods and partly to take advantage of the superb view of the sea with its constantly changing light. The sitting room is a calm, easily maintained space. From the road, the house, originally a barn built in about 1800, appears to be a working farm building typical of Norfolk, with its pebbled exterior, but, invisible except from the sea, French windows lead out onto balconies.

Cricket is England's quintessential country game in summer. Every village in the early 20th century had a cricket club, but today many of these villages have been sucked into towns and the rural spirit that fostered a local cricket club has dwindled. Some cricket pavilions, built to be wonderfully cool and shady, have simply been abandoned. It took an enterprising architect, Alfred Munkenbeck, of Munkenbeck and Marshall, to see possibilities in a 1910 cricket pavilion on the South Downs (shown on page 121 in its restored state), which used to be attached to a private house. An American from Greenwich, Connecticut, Munkenbeck craved airiness and an expansive view, and this pavilion fitted the bill. It was bought in one afternoon after his wife saw an estate agent's advertisement at the doctor's surgery. The Munkenbecks restored and remodeled it into a weekend house, just one hour away from London. Its exterior and verandah are shown on page 182.

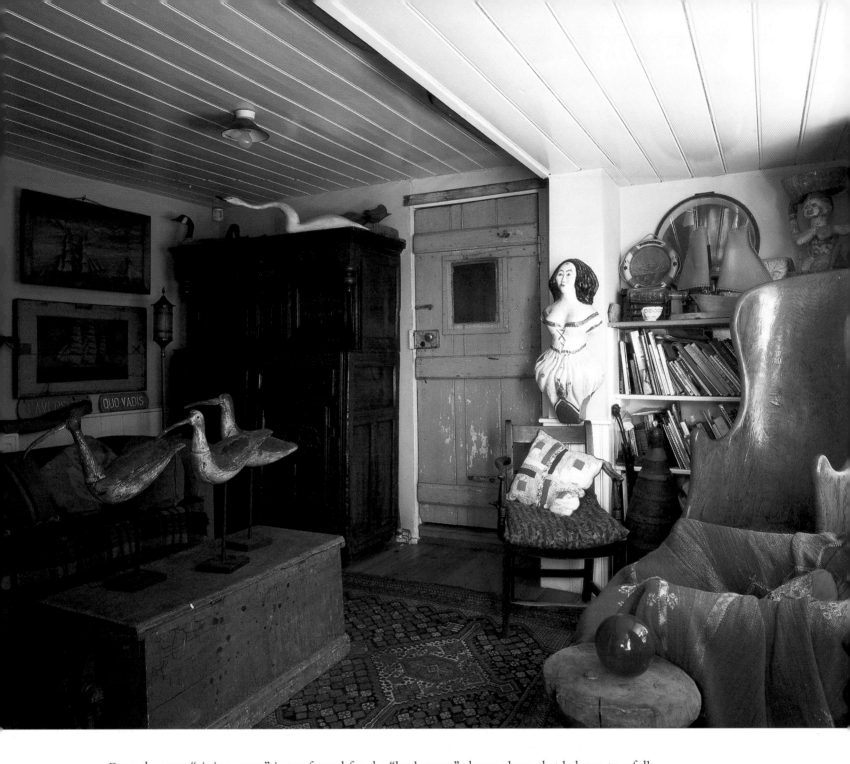

Even the term "sitting room" is too formal for the "back room" shown above that belongs to a folk artist – who specializes in sculpting birds – and his wife. There is a "front room" in the house, used for watching television, but the "back room" was added later and has become filled with folk art and found objects. Starting life in the East End of London, the owner worked as a bird keeper in Regent's Park, but now lives in the country near "loads of artists." The house is filled with nautical pictures and objects – dioramas of boats, "woollies" (scenes embroidered by 19th-century sailors in wool yarn), silk pictures, seaside memorabilia, punt guns for shooting ducks on the river nearby, and driftwood fish. Serendipity and the wear of time on objects – plus a large dose of iconoclastic creativity – combine to make this a delightful English room.

LIBRARIES

BELOW: A masculine dark wine is the overriding color of this classic library in the restored, late Jacobean Harrington Hall in Lincolnshire. The room is anchored by a Ziegler carpet. The house has been so lovingly restored that electric plugs are hidden behind lift-up panels in the skirting boards.

THE ENGLISH, HAVING THE BLESSING OF A DIVERSE LANGUAGE, are famously literate and have an innate love of books. From medieval times, libraries had been revered. The monasteries, and Oxford and Cambridge's colleges, were the main repositories of handwritten and illustrated books. From the mid-15th century, when printed books became available, private libraries increased in number. The library at Eyam Hall, a manor house in the Peak District of Derbyshire, contains a typical English country gentleman's collection. The earliest book dates from 1546, and the volumes include a 1675 anatomy book with hand-colored fold-out sections like today's children's pop-up books.

By the 18th century, the library had become an essential room in a Great House. Aristocrats of the day were educated to read the ancient languages of Latin, Greek and Hebrew, as well as French and Italian. Folios of botanicals, architectural drawings, and maps were collected by those doing the Grand Tour, and suitable rooms were needed to house them. In addition to its Kent-designed long library, Holkham Hall has a smaller octagonal library in the South Tribune with alcoves constructed especially to hold over-sized folios. Kent died before the main library wing was finished but its architectural details (seen on page 126) – split pediments with centered busts over the bookcases, modillion cornice and lozenged plaster ceiling – make it one of the most beautiful English libraries. In the same league is the library at Houghton Hall, also by Kent, and one in a lighter style by Adam at Kedleston Hall.

The library at Sledmere House is not only a book room but also a long gallery, which was built on a monumental scale in the 18th century by the 2nd Baronet, Sir Christopher Sykes, a collector of rare books. The most precious tomes – including two volumes of the Gutenberg Bible – were sold in 1824 because the family needed money following the Napoleonic Wars. Many landed up in the Pierpont Library, New York. In its time the Sledmere library had been used for daily exercise by the 4th Baronet, and later by his daughter-in-law as a drawing room, completely cluttered with furniture – settees, sociables, screens and potted palms – towards the end of the 19th century. The glory of the room, which stretches right across the house, lies in its arched and decorated ceiling, the design echoed in the oak and mahogany parquet floor below.

As the calming lines of Classical symmetry, with its columns and pediments, became the mainstream of mid-18th-century architecture, a counter-movement, starting with literary inspiration and dubbed Gothic – or more fancifully Gothick – took hold among some English aesthetes. Named by the Italians, who viewed the Gothic tribes who had destroyed the Classical art of the Roman empire as barbaric, it was defiantly – even perversely – anti-Classical. Novelist Horace Walpole, fourth son of Sir Robert, started a craze for a romantic interest in Medievalism when he built Strawberry Hill in Twickenham. Chippendale, ever the astute businessman, sensed the trend and produced chairs with Gothick arched backs. Gothick motifs in interiors and furnishings continued well into the Regency period. At Strawberry Hill, fan-vaulted ceilings were produced in plaster rather than stone, giving a theatrical ambience, a feeling that disappeared when Gothick became the Gothic Revival, responding to the serious moralistic tone set during the Victorian era. On page 127 is a library-cum-office with Gothick-inspired decorative embellishments on the

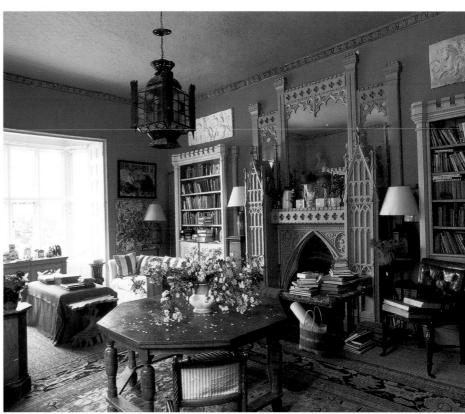

ABOVE: This library-cum-office belongs to garden designers Julian and Isabel Bannerman, who live at Hanham Court near Bristol. The Gothic fireplace was assembled from old church organs and the design is based on the gates at Beckford's Fonthill. The octagonal table is reputed to have been designed by architect Alfred Waterhouse; the lamp above is from Ronda in Andalusia, Spain. Holes in the very worn Ziegler carpet were cut out and the carpet re-pieced. Near the window, an antique blanket box is covered with blankets. Beyond it, architectural models sit in the sun. In a characteristically English way, to help prevent the room from being taken too seriously, the bust on the mantelpiece wears a hat.

LEFT: An example of a splendid library at Holkham Hall in Norfolk, designed by William Kent, who died before it was finished in 1762. Architectural details include split pediments with busts over the shelves, a deeply molded lozenged ceiling, and lots of gilding. The center of the library has been furnished like a drawing room with upholstered sofas and armchairs.

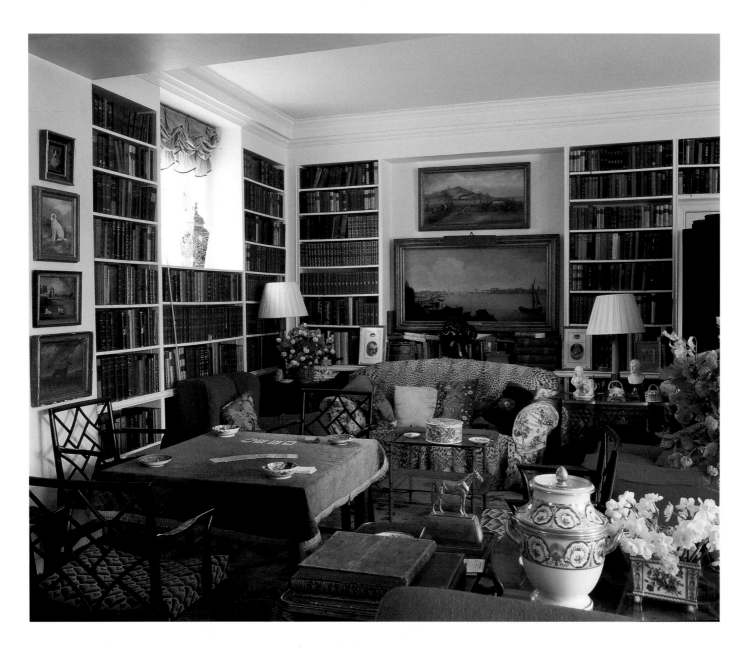

*ABOVE: In this combination of
library, games room and
sitting room belonging to Lord
and Lady Astor, the sofa has a
chintz loose cover, a mixture of
cushions and a fur rug. The
wall-to-ceiling bookcases are
interspersed with paintings.
Balloon shades at the window,
collections of bibelots and
plenty of flowers soften this
comfortable, and typically
English room.*

fireplace, the mirror, and the bookcases. A contemporary version of decorative, twig-formed neo-Gothick can be found in the sitting room *orné* at Harrington Hall (see page 130).

Though libraries in the 17th and 18th century were often used as family rooms, by the 19th and 20th century they had gradually become a male preserve. In manor houses men frequently used the library as a study in which to deal with estate business. The decoration of libraries developed a masculine quality, using dark hunter green, navy, and maroon colors, plenty of leather, tartan, a Turkey (imitation Persian) carpet, and brass lamps with tole (painted or japanned tin) or parchment shades.

Bookcases are the most important design element in a library. The bookcase with glazed doors made an appearance toward the end of the 17th century, as did the bureau-bookcase, veneered in oak or walnut, with drawers below and shelves for books above. The glazed-front bookcase was developed in the 18th century into such splendid pieces as Chippendale's Gothick-style mahogany versions with carved astragals (beaded molding that divided the glass fronts into lozenge and ogee designs) and a pair of pointed arches at the top. In the Regency period, books might be housed in large, plate-glass-fronted bookcases with Classical columns dividing the doors, or in small, freestanding open-shelved rosewood bookcases that were circular or revolving. Some were fronted with brass trellis-work rather like chicken wire. By the late Victorian and Edwardian era, almost every house had some sort of bookcase.

Some libraries have curtaining inside the "chicken-wire" front to protect the books from fading. Library shelves are often edged with tooled leather or felt, cut into pinked scallops, fringes, or V-shapes. This now-decorative device was introduced in the 17th century when books were a luxury: fabric, sometimes cut into fringes, was attached to shelves so that dust was gently removed from the top of the book as it was drawn out. The fabric was sometimes as much as 6 inches (15cm) long, to prevent fading on the spines, but was light enough not to damage them. This device can be seen in the library at Erddig, a grand farmhouse built in the late 17th century in North Wales.

In the modern library, if simple white bookshelves butt up against the wall, the room can get a lift if the wall is painted in a contrasting colour, perhaps a strong sugar-bag blue or coral red. If bookcases do not reach the ceiling, objects are often placed on top of them. In the 18th century, these objects were inspired by the Grand Tour and included busts, urns, obelisks, columns, miniature architectural models, and the much-collected early reproductions of bronzes from the Naples Museum. These still work well today, although there has been a relaxation of the rules of what is considered permissible decoration. Some libraries now have a wonderful clutter of nostalgic and personal objects: 19th-century Portabello pottery lions, 18th-century grotesque jugs, copper lustre dogs, Chinese tobacco jars, Staffordshire figures, model ships in bottles, and family snapshots.

The decorative arrangement of books within bookcases is a talent in itself, but, because such arrangements value the aesthetic more highly than the strictly systematic, it has little appeal for the professional librarian. Small bibelots, precious and whimsical, can be interspersed with books, while oversized books can be laid flat to create pyramids, flanked by books placed upright. Pictures – engravings, watercolors, hunting scenes, Classical landscapes, portraits of people, favorite dogs and horses – or antique porcelain plates can be hung on the shelves' upright studs. In a country library, these decorative arrangements work best if there is controlled asymmetry and signs of a sense of humor.

As libraries grew in importance in the 18th century, special furniture was needed over and above the lecterns and table desks that had been present since the medieval period. The ever-ingenious English cabinet-makers produced many types of ladder to reach books on upper shelves, as well as chairs and stools that converted into steps. Large geographic globes were a favorite item. Library tables became big and sturdy, and held paper weights, a magnifying glass, a paper knife, and sometimes a brass set of scales.

An ideal library may be full of beautiful, antique, leather-bound books, or it may be modern, with collections of recent first editions, but it must display an originality that reflects the owner, and include enough comfort to make for ease, but not so much that the reader is lulled into a soporific state. No matter how big the room, however, there are never enough bookshelves.

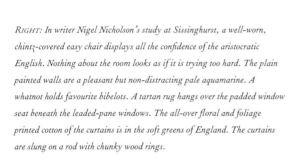

LEFT: The owners of Harrington Hall had a clean slate to work on after the fire that destroyed the interior. They wanted a "Gothick" parlor/study. Decorator Christopher Nevile chose sculptor Oriel Harwood, who designed and brought her team to install this whimsical room made with plaster twigs and cleverly using mirrors to give the impression of space beyond the arches.

RIGHT: In writer Nigel Nicholson's study at Sissinghurst, a well-worn, chintz-covered easy chair displays all the confidence of the aristocratic English. Nothing about the room looks as if it is trying too hard. The plain painted walls are a pleasant but non-distracting pale aquamarine. A whatnot holds favourite bibelots. A tartan rug hangs over the padded window seat beneath the leaded-pane windows. The all-over floral and foliage printed cotton of the curtains is in the soft greens of England. The curtains are slung on a rod with chunky wood rings.

STUDIES

THE STUDY IN A COUNTRY HOUSE is a distinctly English room. Studies are essentially private work rooms which have the intellectual overtones of a library. In a country rectory, the room where sermons are written would be called a study, even if lined with books two deep on the shelves. Bookcases in a study may be filled with scientific, medical, and archeological reference books, with titles on art, design, music, and literature, and with many volumes of a thesaurus, which together form a small working library.

A study also functions as an office and is a place to keep accounts, document records from the past, store old letters and photographs, and even position a safe. It can also be a room for confidential interviews, or where offspring are reprimanded, where parishioners discuss their problems, or patients their symptoms.

A desk or work table is essential. Some tiny studies are practically filled by a large, antique partner's desk – a flat, leather-topped table, well supplied with drawers but with knee spaces on either side so that two people can sit facing each other. This scale of desk, which would have been used originally in a 19th-century office, can bestow an off-beat charm on a small study. Lacquered bureau-cabinets made during the reign of Queen Anne (1702–14) had a desk front that could be let down to reveal cubby holes for writing equipment and cupboards with further small spaces for displaying curios. These fancily decorated pieces were rather more feminine-looking than the average study desk. More common was the walnut-veneered bureau with a sloping top that opened to give a writing desk supported by two pull-out props. During the 18th century, mechanical desks were ingeniously designed with any number of hidden compartments. On these desks there would have been a standish – a dish, often made of silver, that held pens – and an ink well, which might be of cut glass with a silver

ABOVE: In this study, the
garden display designer
George Carter uses a round
table on which to produce his
ideas. The large plaster urns
were made for display
purposes. Crisp stripes
upholster the sofa and chair.
The standing lamp has had
marbled paper stuck onto its
base and a shade made from
wallpaper.

RIGHT: This stylish library/study in the Menagerie belonged to house
historian, the late Gervase Jackson-Stops. Dark green curtains are swagged
to accommodate the arched window. On a table in front of it, sits a stuffed
lemur with a smart striped tail, which reflects the original house's name.
Bookshelves line the high walls, necessitating the library steps seen on the
left. Antique reproductions of Classical statues sit on the ledges. A skylight
at the back of the room lights an entertaining trompe-l'oeil painting of
Gervase at work by Hector MacDonnell.

RIGHT: The studio of abstract painter, the late Patrick Heron, is light and uncluttered. Plain wood floors and white walls provide a background for a work table and chairs that have clean lines inspired by 1950s Scandinavian furniture. On the table, tools are organized. A window seat is used to display a painting.

OPPOSITE: At a far corner of the back garden of Brian Godbold's Elizabethan village row house, an outer barn has been skillfully converted into a photographic studio. At first the neighbors, fearing creeping modernization in this well-preserved street, voiced objections, but now they think it is beautiful.

lid. There would also have been a container of fine sand, which was used to blot wet ink. This was replaced in the 19th century by blotting paper, in pink, green, or pale blue, which came in large sheets and was held on a leather pad by tooled-leather corners, or on a wooden roller.

Writing tools have changed significantly over time. Quill pens – made from the large wing feathers of swans, turkeys, geese, and even black crows – were superseded in the early 19th century by a variety of experimental ideas, including decorated glass pens, pen points made from horn and tortoiseshell, and ornate nibs studded with rubies, as well as early fountain pens. Machine-made steel nibs were invented in England in 1780 and were still in use up until the Second World War, although the ballpoint pen was patented in America in 1888. Some poets, out of bravado or perversity, still choose to compose on vintage typewriters, but today most studies include the ubiquitous computer.

The study is a good place for collections of small objects, for those without libraries or grand passages in which to display their culture. This may consist of a country-pine cupboard with a collection of shells, an ornate, gilded Regency cupboard housing fossils, a framed collection of sealing-wax impressions, or an 18th-century glass-topped relics table displaying curios. Collections of coronation memorabilia or stuffed birds in bell jars might top bookcases, and a cork bulletin board hold clippings, sketches, and postcards.

If collections are displayed too seriously, the room looks like a museum instead of a comfortable, lived-in place. It is worth remembering the English antique dealer's phrase: "Never disturb the original dust," as well as artist Nathalie Barney's remark to the grand *horizontale* Liane de Pougy when they were visiting a grand but very dusty house: "But dust is pretty, it's furniture's face powder."

back rooms

kitchens &
dining rooms

ABOVE: Superbly suited to its architectural shell, this charming, traditionally decorated dining room at the Menagerie reflects the unerring taste and imagination of Gervase Jackson-Stops. The golden glow of the walls and fabrics enhances the barley-sugar-twisted legs of the needlepoint-covered chairs and the collection of exemplary ceramics on the shelves.

LEFT: This kitchen-cum-dining room in interior designer Robert Kime's country house has all the elements needed for comfort; a scrubbed ash table, Windsor chairs made of yew, a stove set in the fireplace, and an 18th-century dresser displaying French 19th-century pottery. The room is given formality by the 1750 brass chandelier and the period-framed pictures on the walls.

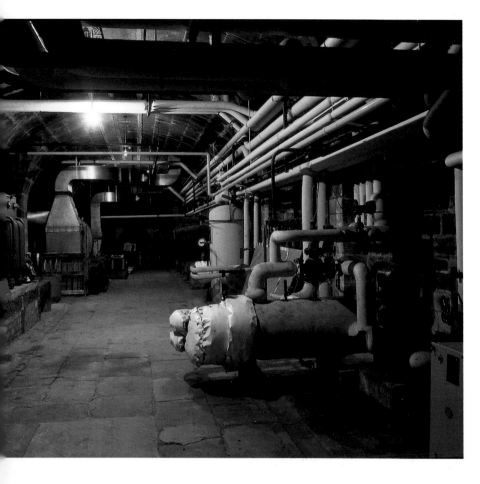

LEFT: Unseen by the general public, the boiler room at Chatsworth in Derbyshire, the huge ancestral home of the Duke of Devonshire, contains the machinery needed to keep a great house going.

RIGHT: An Aga kitchen range – an essential component of the well-appointed country kitchen – with ovens and hot plates, not only provides heat for cooking but also heats the house. Agas fit neatly into the arched fireplaces of houses dating back to Tudor times. Here, the fireplace alcove has been modernized with tiles.

KITCHENS

IN THE COUNTRY, IT IS THE OUTDOOR ENTRANCE nearest to the kitchen that is most frequently used by the family because the kitchen, once the realm of servants, is now the hub of the house. Medieval and Tudor kitchens fascinate us as we try to visualize what it must have been like to work in these large, often dank and dark spaces. At Haddon Hall, worn steps lead to the 14th-century kitchens, which include a butcher's kitchen with a meat-hanging rack and a chopping block concave in the center from hacking. Butteries and kitchens usually led off a medieval hall, such as at Gainsborough Hall, once an isolated medieval stronghold, but now surrounded by houses. At Elizabethan Burghley House, animals skulls – some say of rabbits, others of faithful mousing cats – are arranged on the kitchen wall in a pattern. In Jacobean Eyam Hall, the buttery and dairy were separate buildings, built of the local millstone grit and now converted into a gift shop and a restaurant. Curators of Great Houses display antique kitchen equipment: crocks, pans, pestles-and-mortars, salt and spice boxes, colanders, old bread boards, graters, coffee grinders, jelly molds, butter pats, and pudding basins. Vintage dairy utensils are collected and displayed in modern kitchens, such as the dairy bowls in Nicholas Haslam's flower-arranging room on page 142 and in Brian Godbold's kitchen on page 143. Kitchen utensils are frequently co-opted into kitchen décor, as in the witty use of colanders, a wok, tart and patty pans as light fittings in the kitchen at Harrington Hall.

The kitchen at Erdigg is one of the grandest architecturally, with a big Palladian window and three rusticated arches. When this new kitchen was built in the early 1770s, it was detached from the house to prevent the spread of fire. Erdigg has a bakery that is still used on a regular basis for baking bread

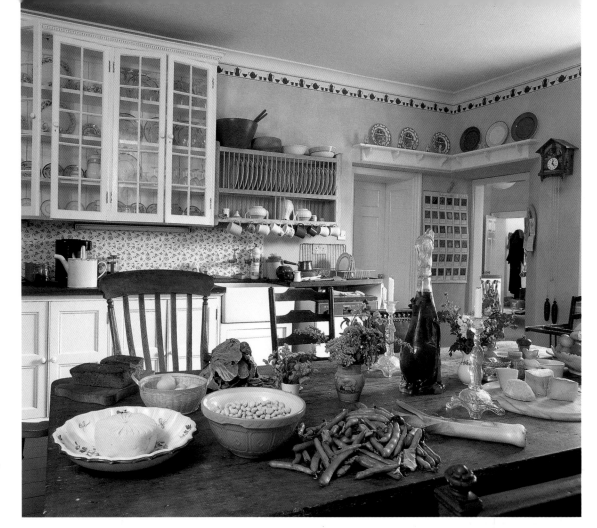

RIGHT: A canny observer will identify the same color scheme and border as in the kitchen on page 51. This picture shows the kitchen in the Castle, a folly on the Sledmere estate where Christopher Simon Sykes and his family gather during the holidays. Meals are cooked and eaten here at the big country table surrounded by a variety of chairs.

in the scuffle ovens. These ovens used to be wood-heated for several hours, after which the ashes were "scuffled-out" onto the floor and the bread was put in on long wooden peels. There is also a scullery for the preparation of meat, vegetables, and fish, as well as for washing dishes, and a still room for distilling cordial waters, medicine, and scents, and for storing sugar, tea, coffee, and preserves. Still rooms in the 19th century were used as places where servants prepared light breakfasts and afternoon tea.

Large houses still have housekeepers and cooks but their place in today's household is very different from what it was in the past. At Badminton House in Gloucestershire, there is an early example of the bell system used to call servants, dating from the first decade of the 17th century, and the rope pulls still have their labels, such as: "Once for Footman; Twice Lampman," and "Once for Groom of the Chamber; Twice for Duke's Valet." In 19th-century houses, the lady of the house embroidered needlepoint bell pulls, which can now be seen in a purely ornamental role in the sitting rooms of many traditionally decorated homes. Later, a numbered buzzer system summoned the required help. If servants were overworked and underpaid, they did not often complain because there were always plenty of others ready to take their places. Right up until the Second World War, many young girls left school at the age of 13 and went "into service at a good house." They started as the lowest paid, to learn the running of the house from the bottom up, and gradually became a fixed part of the servant hierarchy. Their jobs and responsibilities are clearly delineated in the many reprintings of Mrs. Beeton's *Book of Household Management*.

Household inventions have proliferated. Cooking methods evolved from the wood-fueled fireplace with its spit for roasting and kiln bread oven of the medieval period to, by the early 20th century, a much smaller coal-fueled fireplace in the basement kitchen or, in middle-class homes, at the back of the house. The fireplace had a trivet on which a kettle of water was kept hot, while the fire also heated adjacent built-in ovens as well as water in a tank above for use in the bathroom. A new fuel, gas, was introduced in the 19th century. Gas stoves or ranges were clean, convenient, and economic because they could be instantly regulated. Anthracite was another inexpensive fuel used for cooking and in many country kitchens it still fuels one of the most popular cooking ranges in English country houses, the all-purpose Aga, shown on page 139.

ABOVE: A Georgian farmhouse on the Holkham Estate was renovated for a young family by the architect Justin Meath Baker, then with Baker Nevile Design. This kitchen, entered through a walled courtyard, is now the hub of the house. Light woodwork, terracotta tiles and patchwork curtains create a cheerful, country flavor.

LEFT: Arranging flowers in an uncontrived, insouciant way is an amateur pastime dear to English hearts. Here a whole room – filled with basins, blue-and-white mugs on shelves, and baskets arranged on a wall – has been given over to the pursuit. The house, once a Jacobean hunting lodge, is now owned by interior designer Nicholas Haslam, but, until his death in 1977, belonged to decorator John Fowler of Colefax & Fowler. The house was used by set designer Julia Oman Strong for the film Charge of the Light Brigade, *made in the 1960s.*

ABOVE: A pine dresser in this kitchen holds a collection of earthenware, much of it French country pottery. The house belongs to designer/ photographer Brian Godbold and is one of a row of village houses built in Elizabethan times that were later given Georgian fronts.

The first electric light bulb suitable for domestic use was made in 1880, but remote country cottages and farmhouses often remained lit by candles and oil lamps up until the mid-20th century. Electric ovens soon followed, but they were expensive and were only used by a few pioneers until the 1920s. The 1909 edition of Mrs. Beeton's book stated: "the King's yacht (constructed for her late Majesty, Queen Victoria) is fitted up with a complete electric kitchen outfit, including soup and coffee boilers, hot-plates, ovens, grills and hot closets." Today, many kitchens include a late 20th-century invention, the microwave oven, for quick heating.

England's cool climate means that kitchens have never had the same need for refrigeration as those in America: a larder or pantry with a stone slab and shelves above it sufficed for most country houses until the 1950s. Pantries had small windows to keep the room dark and cool. Some also had hanging shelves to thwart mice. To keep milk cool, jugs were set in bowls of cold water and covered with circles of butter muslin weighed down slightly with an edging of beads. Glass butter dishes were made to fit into covered earthenware bowls filled with water, and, for fancy occasions, butter dishes were set in water-filled silver containers with domed lids. Now refrigeration is deemed essential, and in a large household this will also include gigantic freezers for storing cuts of meat and vegetables.

Often the less well-known subsidiary rooms of a great house are fascinating because they show how such a house functions. In country houses today, the butler's pantry is a catch-all name for the place where plates, glassware, and cutlery are stored, although it would originally have been used to hold the liquor brought from the buttery, since the butler was in charge of wines and spirits. The maids' rooms have now been dressed up into extra guest rooms. The scullery, with its terracotta-tiled floor, sink, and drying rack is now usurped by the automatic dishwasher; and the wash-house, with its copper boiler, galvanized tub, washboard, wooden dolly (used to pound clothes) and mangle – and close by outside the washing lines, props, and pegs – have all been superseded by the modern laundry room. This is a shame because the sun and green grass combine to whiten bed linen and make it fragrant. At Eyam the original wash-house contains the well from which all the water used in the Hall itself was once piped. Erddig has wet and dry laundries, one for washing, the other for drying and ironing. Ironing, especially using goffering irons to produce tiny pleats on the starched-lace collars popular in the Elizabethan period, was an admired skill. Country people were still using flat irons heated on t he stove during the Second World War. Now these irons are bought in antique shops for use as paper weights and doorstops.

Seldom-visited rooms include the wine cellar, which, in a great house, can be an elaborate catacomb of stacked bottles, and might have an iron-lined door and a lock protected with sealing wax for security. Antique wine equipment – ice buckets, stoppers, decanters, and silver or Bilston enamel bottle tickets – once the province of wine stewards and butlers, is now highly collectable. The boiler room in the cellars at Chatsworth (see page 138) gives some idea of the mammoth underpinnings needed to operate a huge house.

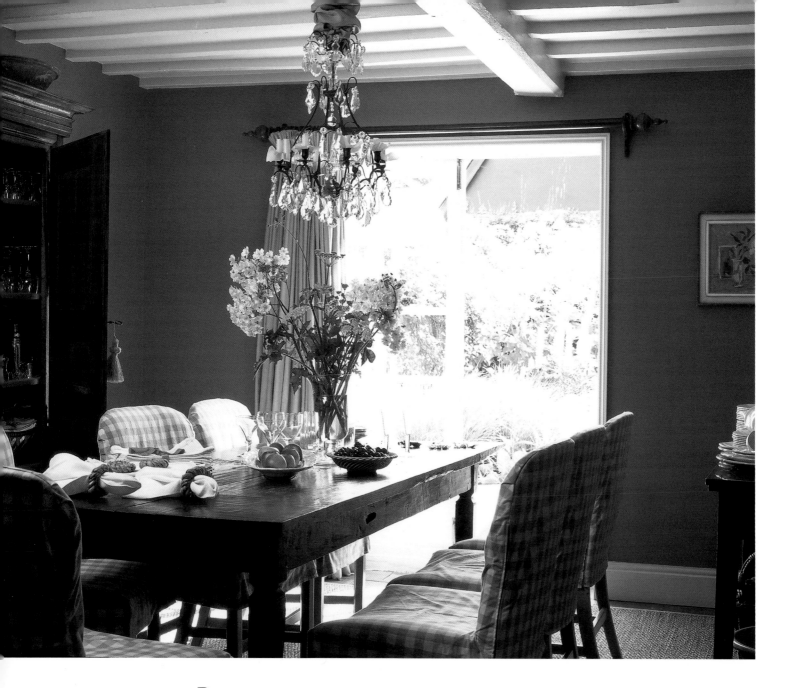

DINING ROOMS

DURING THE MEDIEVAL PERIOD, ENGLISH COUNTRY FEASTS took place in makeshift areas using movable furniture. Trestle tables were easy to transport on journeys from one country estate to another, and could be rearranged according to the number of diners. They would be set up in a U-shape in an all-purpose hall, and a procession of food bearers would bring communal platters in from the kitchen. By the late Tudor period, there had been a move away from the earlier focus on the great hall, previously the main room for elaborate dining. At Elizabethan Hardwick Hall the dining room is placed two floors up from the kitchen, and so the food must have been stone cold when it arrived at the table. This was, however, a rather unusual arrangement, possibly adopted by Bess of Hardwick to emphasize her modern outlook, or to demonstrate a better view of her property. In either case, it would have been made with complete disregard for the servants, who had to carry up laden platters. Tables in Elizabethan dining rooms were made from oak and were very heavy, with elaborately carved bulbous legs held at the bottom by stretchers; buffets with shelves stood against the walls.

Most 17th-century dining rooms were situated on the ground floor, with the kitchen conveniently nearby or in the basement below. As the size of the great hall shrank, however, the dining room gained in importance until, at the end of the 18th century, in the pursuit of grandeur, it had moved far away from the kitchen and food frequently had to be carried along numerous cold passages.

In grand 18th-century English country houses built in the Georgian style, a great dining room would have been used for major festivities with, by now, a permanent central table that could be lengthened with additional leaves. Small groups, on less formal occasions, ate in a separate dining parlor. Drawings of the dining rooms of this time often show pairs of large urns that would have been filled with water to rinse wine glasses. Now these are used simply for decoration. At the end of a large meal, men preferred to remain around the table to talk and drink port, and the ladies retired to a drawing room. So engrossing was the all-male conversation that a "piss pot" was often placed nearby, usually behind a screen or in a cupboard-like alcove, so that conversation could continue uninterrupted.

ABOVE: This folksy eating room, once the old kitchen, was only half this size until the owners added a back wing to their house. Chairs from a Welsh farmhouse surround the poorhouse table. A wood pigeon decoy sits in a bowl. The cupboard is Scandinavian. Nautical motifs abound, including the boat on the ceiling, sculpted sea birds and driftwood fish.

OPPOSITE: Above the mantelpiece in Christopher Gibbs's dining room, a molded, ebonised and giltwood frame encloses a watercolor copy of designs by Sir Joshua Reynolds for a stained-glass window at New College, Oxford. It depicts the Nativity; one of the shepherds is a portrait of Reynolds himself. The three-screen fireguard is made from pieces of old oriental chintz.

The dining room at Sledmere House in Yorkshire (see page 150) is an impressive example from the 18th century. Its 1751 plasterwork ceiling was made by York plasterers using a robust, heavily molded style typical of the mid-Georgian period, but the walls, designed in 1787, show the lighter Adam manner and were done by Joseph Rose, the most famous plasterer of the day. When the dining room is open to the public, the table is surrounded by fine 1760 Chinese-style Chippendale chairs. The chairs shown around the table in this photograph are in a simpler mid-18th-century style, and there is yet another set of sturdier chairs used for shooting lunches. English country houses were not known for having the best cuisine, but Sledmere has long enjoyed a reputation for good food, much of it produced right on the estate.

Despite the grandeur of dining rooms in England's great country houses, most people lived less ostentatious lives, using rooms on a scale similar to the one shown on page 136, with its scrubbed ash table and elm Windsor chairs. This style of chair has been a staple of country rooms since 1750. It was often made from a variety of woods found locally: elm for the seat, beech for the spindles, and ash or yew for the back rails. Late 18th-century farmhouses had enormous kitchens with plain plaster walls and oak-beamed ceilings, and this was where the family ate, often continuing to use pewter plates from an earlier era. As in town, today many country dining rooms are only used for dinner parties and special occasions. Like farming people in the past, families who have a large enough kitchen use it for most meals, often eating around a scrubbed wooden table.

The dining room in a Regency parsonage would have been modest, but, certainly in the past, it would have been used by the family for all the meals, which were always served by a maid, no matter how impoverished the parson. The room would have been wallpapered with a striped pattern, possibly with dainty flowers interspersed. In a more sophisticated house, the wallpaper might have had an arabesque design of delicate, interlaced curlicues incorporating urns, medallions, Classical figures, and acanthus leaves. Turkey carpets were placed on the wooden floor but would probably only have been fitted wall to wall in a smart Regency town house.

Throughout England, rooms became more filled with furniture as the 19th century progressed, but fashions were slower to change in the country and dining rooms usually remained simple, finally being regarded as charmingly old-fashioned. Today, if a formal dining room has no special architectural features, hanging wallpaper with some drama and a reasonably large-scale pattern, helps to set the scene. Antique scenic panels might be appropriate, or a Chinese paper with trees, flowers, and birds, or the mottled antique silver paper that once lined tea crates. Dining rooms are wonderful places for *trompe-l'oeil* murals, which help to expand the space.

In most stately homes that are open to the public, the dining room is a set piece of formality. Unless the dining room is rented out for weddings or corporate events, the table is laid with the house's most impressive china and silver. The table may be covered with a white linen cloth, often with a damask weave, starched and ironed to just the right degree. In the medieval period, the tablecloth, which hung low around the table to hide the trestles, was used to wipe the hands and mouth like a napkin. Individual

napkins were a later development, probably introduced in the Tudor age. Georgian napkins were much larger than those we use today – big enough to tie around the neck – and in Victorian times some had a button-hole to attach to a shirt button.

Creases were deliberately ironed into tablecloths in the 14th century, vertically and horizontally, to give a decorative effect, and sometimes they had knots tied in the corners. Nowadays, some households store their tablecloths on rollers to avoid creases. Though white napery with colored embroidery or threads woven into it has been used since the 13th century, or possibly earlier, solid colors for tablecloths and napkins only made a general appearance in the late 19th century. Printed cloths and napkins came into use in the 1940s, and their mid-century designs are now coveted. A luxurious but practical contemporary idea is to cover the table with a quilted cloth, and place a smaller square cloth on top to take the brunt of wear.

The main focus of the dining room is the enticing table, and the English are connoisseurs of china. This does not mean that every plate has to match: the English are good at making a feature of necessity and some of the most interesting tables are laid with a variety of plates, which can become a fascinating topic of conversation. Even experts are forgiving of the occasional chipped plate if it is a beauty – and they can get quite excited by 18th-century plates that have been repaired in the style of the time with metal bars on the back. The English also take antique silver seriously and can be similarly knowledgeable about hallmarks on cutlery, all of which may be happily mismatched on the table, providing it is well polished. In the Victorian period, this was the butler's job in a grand house and, owing to the damp weather, it is still a weekly chore in some households. Old glasses are also admired, from simple 18th-century tavern

wine glasses to elaborately cut and gilded Edwardian long-stemmed glasses. Many English people feel an intrinsic love of these objects and use them with pleasure, despite the fact that they cannot be replaced.

Arranging a table is a special skill. The English in the country like to use what is to hand: flowers from the garden or field. The flowers should never look bought or arranged by a florist. Each family has their own way of making a table personal. Some place tiny stacks of antique bound books – titles selected for the group at hand – and arrange flowers in collections of tiny vials and antique scent bottles among them. When Cecil Beaton lived at Ashcombe in Wiltshire in the 1930s – a remote country house that he furnished almost on his wit alone – he described with joy how he had arranged dandelion clocks in a glass bell jar for a dinner party, dashing out to the field with a jam jar to protect each fragile seed head.

ABOVE: George Carter, a garden display designer, makes Classical shapes – urns, swags, obelisks – and uses them in a Post-Modern way throughout his farmhouse. The chairs in his dining room came from his great-grandparents. In the right corner is a headless plaster figure rescued from an art school.

151

upstairs

landings, bedrooms & bathrooms

ABOVE: Plain ochre walls, with marbleizing below the dado, serve as a traditional neutral background for a mixture of old maps and drawings of monuments in Gervase Jackson-Stops's bathroom at the Menagerie.

LEFT: Traditionally English in the John Fowler style, the grand pagoda-topped four-poster bed with a canopy and pleated dust-ruffle was designed by Sally Metcalf. The armchair and curtains are of George Spencer chintz. A vintage white quilt covers the bed and a Porthault dressing gown hangs on the bathroom door.

LEFT: The walls on this staircase at Little Sodbury are decorated with engravings in matching frames, which look almost as symmetrical as wallpaper. It is a look reminiscent of the 18th-century fashion for "print rooms."

LANDINGS

THE STAIRCASE IN A GREAT HOUSE OR COUNTRY MANOR HOUSE is usually larger and grander than those in the more cramped spaces of town houses. At Haddon Hall in Derbyshire, the four curved steps leading to the Long Gallery are said to have been cut from a solid piece of oak from the Haddon grounds, the rest of the tree being used for the floor of the gallery itself. The Great Staircase at Knole in Kent, also Elizabethan, not only has carved beasts on the newel posts but the staircase banisters and posts are also echoed in paint on the walls, in an early example of *trompe l'oeil*.

The remarkably well-preserved Jacobean staircase at Aubourn Hall (opposite) has three flights and shows the extravagant workmanship of the British craftsmen of the day. On the ground floor, there is even a gate to stop dogs running upstairs. Eyam Hall in Derbyshire has a smaller oak staircase, built in 1671, with proportionately smaller stalactite- and stalagmite-esque wood-carving. A practical detail has been added at Eyam, where the bottom step of the staircase is made of stone so that, when the flagstone floor of the hall passage was washed, the step would not rot from constant dousing with water.

Staircases and landings provide a perfect stage for "state and parade." In great houses, the grandeur of the staircases is quite astonishing. At Sudbury Hall in Derbyshire, an impressive cantilevered flight of stairs has a pine balustrade with luxuriant scrolled acanthus leaves, carved in 1675 by Edward Pierce, a craftsman who worked on many of Sir Christopher Wren's churches. On the newel posts are carved baskets of flowers, specially made to be removed and replaced by lamps at night. The ceilings have elaborate fruit and flower plasterwork, framing Classical paintings.

Stairway ceilings painted at the height of the Baroque movement, in the mid-17th century, "beckon mere mortals to ascend and gain the heights of Parnassus," as Gervase Jackson-Stops wrote about Petworth House in West Sussex, where, "a whirlpool of fluttering draperies and limbs, billowing clouds,

ABOVE: The well-preserved, carved oak Jacobean staircase at Aubourn Hall spans three flights. At the bottom, the oak door to prevent dogs from going upstairs is part of the original staircase.

155

RIGHT: *The sea-green staircase contrasts with the marine-blue walls of the Cowpers' landing. Bedrooms — two on this floor — and a sitting room lead off this dramatically curved passage.*

ABOVE: *Architect Chris Cowper of Cowper Griffiths Associates designed his own weekend retreat on the Norfolk coast. Using colors in a way not usually identified with architects, Cowper designed this spectacular first-floor landing to resemble the prow of a ship. The staircase leads up to an attic bedroom.*

and fitful sunbursts" was created by Louis Laguerre. This French artist worked at several of England's great country houses, including Chatsworth. William Kent himself painted the murals in the stair hall at Houghton Hall in Norfolk, but in a more subdued manner borrowed from Palladian Classicism, although his work became more dramatic with the design of the curved white stairs in the Marble Hall at Holkham, which are surrounded by fluted columns of Derbyshire alabaster. He never lived to see the final effect, which is reminiscent of spectacular film sets. Arthur Young, an 18th-century agriculturist and writer, observed with some truth that the space looks like a great bath waiting to be filled.

In the 18th century, whether the landing was a long passage with bedrooms branching off it or a central square, it was used, together with the staircases, to display statues in niches or heavily framed family portraits, and possibly a Tiepolo-esque *trompe-l'oeil* ceiling. While on the Grand Tour – a popular pursuit for the wealthy during this century – many people collected sets of engravings of paintings, allegories, and Classical architectural details. These were either framed and hung, as seen on the staircase at Little Sodbury on page 154, or attached straight onto plain painted walls often of a straw colour or, more rarely, pale blue, green, or pink. A cousin to this form of wall decoration was the print room, a fashion of the 18th and early 19th century. This was usually a separate room, although a recent resurgence of interest in the idea has led to passages, staircases, powder rooms, and bathrooms being used. To create the effect, decoratively printed bands of paper are cut out and pasted over the edges of the engraving, with carefully mitered corners to give the appearance of a frame. The pictures are arranged symmetrically and sometimes connected by cut-out printed garlands, ribbons, ropes, or chains, and embellished with lions' heads, tassels, or fancy ribbon bows. Some of these early print rooms still exist, such as the Caricature Room at Calke Abbey, with its political cartoons by Gilray and Cruikshank, dating from the turn of the 19th century. In more modest houses, the walls of staircases and landings may be covered with colorful botanical prints in period frames, or antique maps.

The landings are the most spectacular part of Chris and Julia Cowper's sea-coast retreat in Norfolk. Chris worked solo on the design of the house. He knew the area, which is flat but untamed, and decided to buy a semi-derelict pebbled barn, built in about 1800, from the Holkham Hall estate. It had only two massively thick walls still reasonably intact. An open breezeway, where once a hay wagon would have been housed, divided the ground floor. On one side is an enclosed space used as a garage and for boat storage. On the other, a door sheltered in the passage leads to the modern kitchen and hall. Above, the house reunites into one long space. An unexpectedly sleek, vivid sea-green staircase curves up to the first floor, where a dramatic landing passage with marine-blue walls looms like the prow of a ship, giving glimpses into bedrooms on the way. The sitting room (see page 120) is also on this floor. A gap in the swerving blue wall has a steep staircase leading to the children's attic room. The colors are amazingly daring and unexpected in an architect-generated scheme. Many architects, raised in the International Style, feel that one color is one too many in a room, but Cowper maintains that this is because all the photographs in the 1920s, when the Bauhaus was at its peak, were in black and white. "The use of color in architecture," he says, "is a lost art." The result of his unorthodox design is exhilarating.

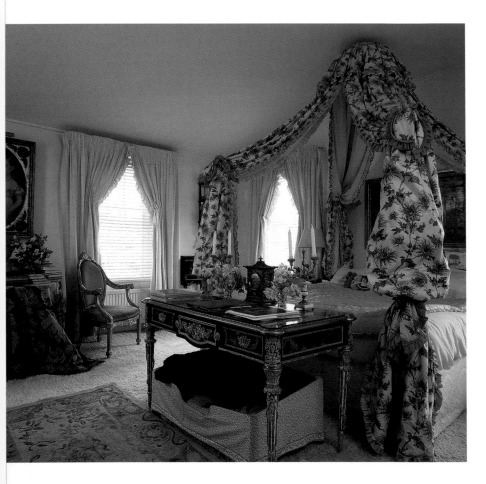

RIGHT: In the school of not so much shabby chic but making a virtue of erudite old fabric, this bedroom is a textile historian's dream. It belonged to Christopher Gibbs. At the back of the bed, is a 17th-century Mughal fabric with a poppy design. The 18th-century coverlet is embroidered with a tree-of-life design. The four-poster bed is in le Style Adelaide *(1830s) and made from Mason's Ironstone ceramic decorated with flowers and acanthus foliage. It is hung with much-repaired, painted satin curtains, probably dating from the 1940s or 1950s.*

ABOVE: This pretty and feminine bedroom in William and Annabel Astor's house in Berkshire has a bed dressed in floral chintz which looks colorful against the cream background of the curtains, ceiling, bed linen and carpet. Tapestry cloth is used on a side table. At the foot of the bed, under a Louis XV boulle bureau plat *table, their dog sleeps in a basket.*

printing of pastoral, historical, or political scenes. This type of design is now called *toile de Jouy* because it developed into a form of art at Jouy-en-Josas in France, supported by the rich and well-connected at Versailles.

Chintz was given a distinctive glazed finish that made it particularly practical for curtaining and upholstery, as it shed dirt easily. Quantities of chintz may be used in English bedrooms, both in town and country, for window and bed curtains, upholstery, and even on walls. The bedrooms shown on pages 71, 152, and above all contain chintz. The fabric has come in and out of fashion for the past 300 years, and no doubt will be back in full force when taste-makers turn away from geometrics and neutral coloring.

Essential furniture in a fashionable French bedroom of the late 17th and early 18th century included the "triad," which consisted of a table flanked by two large candle stands and a looking glass. The ensemble was taken up in a few super-smart English bedrooms, and surviving examples include the rare silver suite at Knole in Kent, dating from about 1676–81, which epitomizes the splendor of English Baroque country houses. Triads were normally set against a pier between two windows, and the mirror was usually tilted downward, unlike the small mirrors found on dressing tables.

By the 18th century, great country houses were designed with separate chambers for the lord and lady. In an aristocratic family, it would have been considered uncivilized for a husband and wife to share one bedroom, though this did not apply to the so-called lower classes. This separation led to the development of the woman's bedroom as frilly and feminine. Grand houses also had a dressing room at the back of the bedroom, which in the *mondaine* world of France was fashionably decorated for entertaining callers.

LEFT: Only in an English room, perhaps, would you find a diminutive child's bed juxtaposed with large, old, family portraits on the walls. The portraits include one of Major John Wright (1724–79) with his brother and sister, and their father, John, as a boy. This room shows the remains of an earlier house that had belonged to a yeoman named John Wilson. Though originally known as the cook's room and part of the servants' quarters, this bedroom at Eyam Hall in Derbyshire now displays vintage toys, such as an 1890 rocking horse made by Ayres, a doll's pram, children's books, Victorian embroidered children's underclothing, and a 1850 dolls' house.

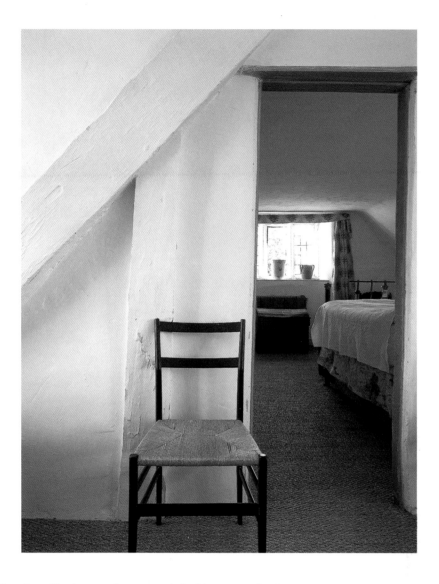

By the 19th century, in contrast to the man's rather frugal bedroom, the woman's had become a frothy agglomeration of lace boudoir pillows, needlepoint slippers and cushions, paisley shawls, cut-work and pin-pricked cardboard lampshades, repoussé silver-backed hair brushes, curling tongs, and scent bottles. Walls were papered with pretty floral designs or in delicate stripes with borders. A bedside mat – perhaps a turkeywork rug in wealthy households – prevented her from stepping out of bed onto a cold wooden floor. Depending on the size of the room, essential furnishings could consist of a chaise longue for reclining, a slipper chair (which had a low seat so that ribbons or buckles on footwear could be easily fastened), a boudoir chair by the bed, on which to fold clothes, an armoire and a chest of drawers.

In the following century, when marriages of all classes were at least in theory more about love than the merging of fortunes, the bedroom was once again shared by husband and wife. It was then dubbed the "master bedroom" by property dealers – a term now amended to "owner's bedroom." Bedrooms that are decidedly late 20th century can look quite at home in older buildings. When artists Douglas Patterson and Joanna Buxton transformed an 1856 Methodist chapel into their home (see page 166), they added an upstairs gallery, mounted on columns to complement the main room, and opened up the ceiling. It was here, on the landing, that they placed their bedroom, with their bed right on the floor.

ABOVE: The walls of this attic bedroom at Hanham Court were stripped down, re-plastered, then given 17 coats of lime wash to achieve a wonderful quality of light. The 1950s chair is by Gio Ponti. The room has been kept perfectly simple with a sisal carpet and a Victorian iron bedstead.

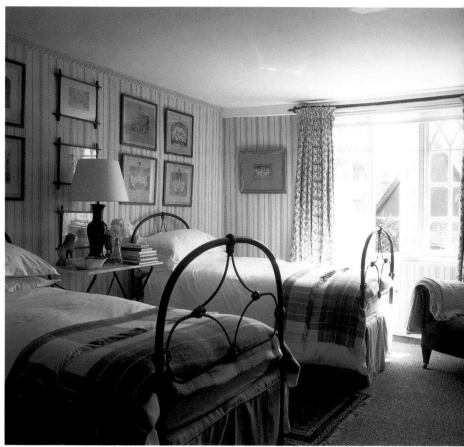

ABOVE: *This pretty and practical village house bedroom contains iron beds which were found at Ben's Bed Bazaar in Framlingham, Suffolk. The wallpaper, its border and all the fabrics are from Colefax & Fowler.*

LEFT: This bedroom in a Georgian farmhouse, renovated by architect Justin Meath Baker, was given bright coloring to appease the demands of the owner's wife when she was pregnant. Ever since, it has been known as the "pregnancy room." Sheer pink curtains decorated with gold and silver thread hang on the simple metal-frame bed. The lithograph with hearts on the wall is by the American artist, Jim Dine.

RIGHT: This beamed attic bedroom at Harrington Hall is used by the daughter of the house. The cotton lawn hangings have been decorated by her with gold spray paint and blue blobs inspired by a Designer's Guild pattern. The 16th-century bed is made of oak. A pewter-colored rod and rings support the drapery which has been casually thrown over a beam above. Oak steps lead up to the bed.

ABOVE: When architect/ designer Douglas Patterson and his wife, artist Joanna Buxton, converted a mid-Victorian Suffolk Methodist Chapel into their country house, they added a gallery floor reached by a spiral staircase. Designed to be used as a simple, pared-down sleeping loft, a bathroom was added on the same floor.

The fashion for four-poster beds petered out in the Victorian period because it was deemed unhygienic to sleep inside a stuffy space. Four-posters have, however, been resurrected in affluent times because they make a bedroom look lavish. The beds shown on pages 160 and 164 are both modern takes on the four-poster, with hangings that are light and merely decorative. Late Victorian farmhouses had rattling brass beds and mattresses filled with feathers – the "feather bed" that was deliciously warm but not as good for the lumbar regions as a firm mattress.

To warm the bed prior to the 20th century, warming pans filled with hot coals were tucked into the bottom end of the bed. The large, heavy stoneware hot-water bottle took its place, to be followed in the 1920s by a rubber version, still used occasionally. Bed linens have also undergone changes. In the 17th and 18th century, the wealthy traveled with their own sheets to make sure that they always had clean linen. Traditionally, sheets were made from white linen for the rich and from hemp for those less well-off. In the 19th century, young girls filled their "bottom drawer," or "hope chest" in preparation for marriage with hand-embroidered sheets, coverlets, and pillowcases. In the 1950s, colored sheets were introduced, later printed with designs, but perhaps nothing beats the feel of well-worn, well-ironed, unadorned cotton sheets.

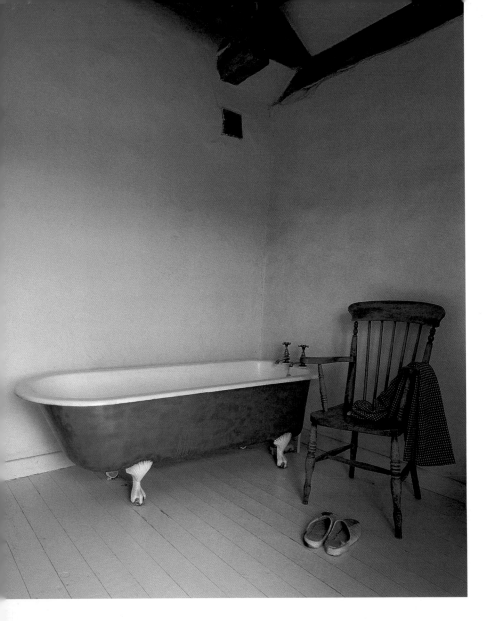

LEFT: This intentionally austere bathroom in a country house in Herefordshire almost reaches the simplicity of a Japanese bathroom but uses traditional English furnishings and a different aesthetic design.

RIGHT: When Julian and Isabel Bannerman came to Hanham Court, they found the bathrooms furnished with pink bathroom suites that were far from their own tastes. This attic bathroom, almost Spartan in its rural simplicity, was created from scratch using a vintage bath on feet and an old-fashioned pedestal sink found at an architectural salvage yard. As with their attic bedroom seen on page 163, the walls were lime-washed, but the bathroom floorboards were left unfinished. The four pictures found their way here because, as so often happens with attics, there was nowhere else to put them.

BATHROOMS

ENGLISH COUNTRY HOUSES USED TO BE NOTORIOUS for their sparse number of bathrooms. Though there may have been splendid ancestral portraits all the way up the stairs, when it came to the amenities, much was lacking. Even in the mid-20th century, guests at a weekend house party would often have to line up in the corridor, sponge bag in hand, waiting their turn. By the time you reached the bathroom, the hot water was already used up, added to which it was a regular practice to leave a window open at all times, no matter how cold the weather. It was not unknown for ice crystals to form on toothbrushes. The idea of heating a bathroom was considered outrageously profligate by the average English home owner. Visitors who complained were considered to be self-indulgent, as "living by the fleshpots of Egypt too long."

Most houses in Europe did not have a room set aside for taking baths until the 19th century, though there might have been an external bath house in large country houses. Most people during the 16th and 17th century washed in their bed-chamber, using a basin and a ewer of water. Despite the spaciousness and luxury introduced at Knole by the 1st Earl of Dorset, who remodeled the house in 1603–08, this was all he used for his ablutions. London had become the soap capital of the world by the 14th century, but in the country soap continued to be made from animal fat and wood ash mixed with herb-based scents until the late 19th century.

ABOVE: *This luxurious guest bathroom at the newly restored Harrington Hall is only for the uninhibited, according to the owner. The bath is next to a large window looking out over the gardens and countryside. With its mirrored walls, some visitors feel quite exposed.*

LEFT: *When planning this commodious bathroom, Christopher Nevile visited a resource for vintage baths and chose the very largest and the very smallest to accommodate an adult and a child at the same time. The mother-and-daughter baths are set aslant in the room, which also includes an amusing, old-fashioned chaise perché with an overhead tank, and a vintage washstand with shelf and mirror. The bare boards are softened by an oriental carpet.*

ABOVE: The free-standing bath in Christopher Gibbs's bathroom has been painted maroon so that it blends in with the oriental carpet. The traveling cupboard on the right, painted by a Circassian slave, belonged to an English explorer and could be knocked down into flat pieces for easy transportation. An English 18th-century chaise perché *can be seen behind the bath.*

Washstands made an appearance in bedrooms in the early 18th century. These were easily moved tripods of wood, holding a small (no more than 10-inch/25-cm wide) ceramic basin and a bottle, with small drawers below for soap and toilet articles. From about 1760, the washstand was an essential piece of furniture in the fashionable bedroom. Some were designed to fit into corners, while others were small cupboards closed with doors, and some were fitted with mirrors. By the mid-19th century, the washstand was being designed en suite with the dressing table and had a marble top and splash tiles, sometimes with a cupboard below, and a matching set of basin, jug, jars, and a soap dish.

Baths were taken only occasionally in the early 18th century, using a portable metal tub of tin or copper placed in the bedroom and filled with heated water carried up from the kitchen in huge cans by servants. It was not until the end of the century, when wigs, powdering, and the use of heavy scents to disguise body odors had gone out of style, that bathing took place with any regularity and was considered a matter of hygiene. Full-length baths were still rare, however, until the end of the 19th century. Some hand-held shower arrangements, attached to the bath taps, were introduced at a similar period, and an early, portable shower, dating from the Edwardian period (1901–10), can be seen at Erddig in North Wales.

When the bathroom did take its place as an essential room in the English country house, after 1850, new watertight and steamproof floors and walls had to be considered. Tiles were, and still are, the most efficient type of flooring. At Sledmere in Yorkshire, a complete Turkish bath was installed as a memorial to Sir Mark Sykes, an expert on the Ottoman Empire, who died in the early 20th century. Most bathrooms were less colorful, however, with white tiles on the walls and terrazzo-style black-and-white tiles on the

floor. A more economical floor covering was linoleum, available in rather loud patterns in the 1880s but with better designs by 1900 as it gained in popularity. Oilcloth was even cheaper, though not as hard wearing.

Ancient Crete had a version of the flushing toilet, but such devices did not develop in modern Europe until the 18th century. English medieval castles had privies, usually in the side turrets, which emptied into the surrounding moat. Tudor and Jacobean houses had a "close stool," a box-like structure holding a chamber pot under an open seat. A well-preserved example can be seen at Knole in the King's Closet, its seat covered in faded crimson velvet with a hinged lid to cover it. In the 19th century, this piece of furniture was called a "commode," a confusing name because it also referred to an elaborate 17th-century cap for women, a small chest of drawers, and a movable washstand with a cupboard. There is still no perfectly apt name for the place used for bodily elimination. All the names used are either slang words, archaic or army terms, or euphemisms: the English word "lavatory" (from the French *laver)* means a washbasin to an American plumber, as it originally did in England in the Tudor period; the word "toilet" implies washing and gussying up; "water closet" was shortened to "W.C." in the mid-20th century, but is less often heard today; the "crapper," honoring the inventor, sounds crude, as does the "head" (a boat term), and "bog," derived from the outhouse of the 18th and 19th century; "powder room" and "little girl's room" both sound coy; the term "toilet" is used in the United States for public labeling, but this becomes "the john" at home.

Britain experienced considerable deprivation during the Second World War, compared to what it was used to. Soap was rationed, toilet paper was often unobtainable, and 3 inches (7–8cm) was the allowable height of water in a bath – even in Buckingham Palace. England took longer than most other countries to recover, but the post-War 1960s affluence resulted in comfortable bathrooms and more of them. The bedroom with a bathroom en suite, though it existed in well-appointed houses, was a new concept for the average country dweller. Bathrooms often had to be concocted out of other rooms or wedged into odd spaces, giving them a charming quirkiness. Some kept the original Spartan look (see, for instance, pages 168 and 169), while others were furnished more like a bed-sitting room with a turkey carpet, an armoire, and an antique *chaise perché*, to give the loo the appearance of a chair.

In the Norfolk farmhouse owned by designer Christopher Nevile, a larder has been transformed into a downstairs loo (see page 175). In the same house, he introduced freestanding mother-and-daughter baths, choosing the largest and the smallest baths available and lining them up side by side as an amusing idea in anticipation of a new arrival (see page 170). In Christopher Gibbs's erudite bathroom (see page 172), which dates from his time at the Manor House at Clifton Hampden, a maroon bath in the middle of the room holds an accessory that is remembered from many English childhoods, the wooden bath rack encrusted with years of soap. The painted cupboard – designed to be collapsible – belonged to Sir Samuel White Baker, an English 19th-century explorer. It was painted by his wife, a Circassian slave whom he had bought in a Turkish slave market. When he brought her back to England, Queen Victoria refused to receive Lady Baker at court because of her past as a slave girl.

The sitting room effect of these rooms is possible because taking a bath causes less steam than a shower and is far kinder to the books, wallpaper, pictures, and collections, which can range from Gosse china seaside memorabilia to bottles of colored sand from the Isle of Wight, often found in country bathrooms. Antique Regency Gothick hanging wall cupboards are now used as medicine cabinets. Bathroom stools with cork seats from the 1920s, or Lloyd loom chairs, hold towels and dressing gowns. Even the toothbrush holders are enamel mugs, perhaps commemorating Queen Victoria's 60 Glorious Years.

In simple village houses, it is only since the 1960s that more than one bathroom has been incorporated, while up until the mid-20th century houses in farming and coal-mining areas, especially in the Midlands and the North, had only outside lavatories. Miners, who often lived in small stone cottages, washed the coal dust off in a tin bath in front of the kitchen stove, but the rest of the family was allowed only one bath a week. That era is now in the past. Many of these tiny cottages have been transformed from houses that held large families into bijou second homes for city folk, with every "mod con."

ABOVE: This room in a restored Georgian farmhouse — now the downstairs loo — was once a larder. There are even special holes for jam pots. The shelves now hold magazines and the walls are lined with school and regimental photographs. The patina of distressed paint has been deliberately preserved as a design statement.

chapter 8

outdoors

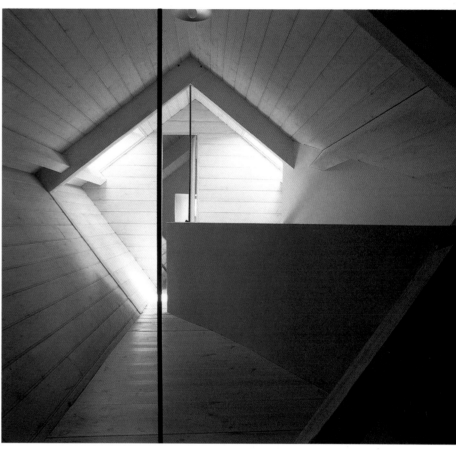

conservatories, lofts, stables & follies

ABOVE: An attic bedroom is a perfect hideaway for children. This one, in a Norfolk barn has a romantic, boyish quality, ideal for the owners' two sons. End-to-end beds are fitted under the sloping roof; they are formed from two Ikea futons on a platform. The room is lined with tongue-and-groove boarding.

LEFT: At Hambledon Hall, a huge glass dome brings plenty of light into this conservatory dining room. Awning-style striped curtains can be closed for privacy. The same striped material is used for the tablecloth on the circular table. Garden-style chairs are fitted with comfortable seat pads. A trellis holds climbing plants; other plantstands include one decorated with rams' heads and another formed from halberds.

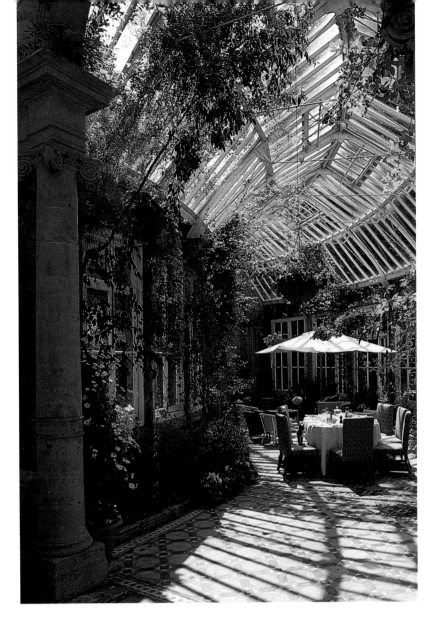

RIGHT: Interior decorator Charles Beresford added this conservatory onto his country house, giving stylish panache to what was originally one of several simple West Sussex chalk workers' farmhouses built in 1912. Preferring the house to look more 1845s in style, Mr. Clark added subtle detailing in the form of flattened arches to all the windows. The little hexagonally topped table with its Gothic overtones and the quatrefoil decorated plant tubs help to foster this period illusion, as do all the neatly clipped hedges and topiary in the garden outside.

ABOVE: The conservatory shown here is in the form of a curved, high-ceilinged corridor that can be used for meals. Rather than installing blinds above, the table has been given a sun umbrella.

A CONSERVATORY IS A LARGE GREENHOUSE DESIGNED for the cultivation and display of plants that would not otherwise survive in the English climate. Glass houses, as they are sometimes called, may have been inspired by orangeries but they proliferated because of a surge of scientific interest in botany in the 18th and 19th century. Botany was not only a popular scientific subject, it was also ideally suited to women as well as men. Mary Delany, who seemed to know everyone in society in the 18th century and was famous for her shell grottoes, was also renowned for her botanically accurate cut-paper flower mosaics. Throughout the 19th century and into the Edwardian era women painted watercolors of flowers, fruit, and vegetables, many of them exceptionally beautiful.

The conservatory's original purpose as a laboratory for plants was modified during the 19th century, when it became a roofed cutting garden that furnished a constant supply of flowers for arranging in the house. Large greenhouses also exist on big estates, as they did in the Victorian period, but these are often testing places for certain species away from the main house and much more utilitarian in design, with shallow trays of plants on shelves and narrow walks between them. In its present form, the conservatory attached to the house has become a plant-filled room used for entertaining and as a setting for meals, whether lunch, dinner, or tea.

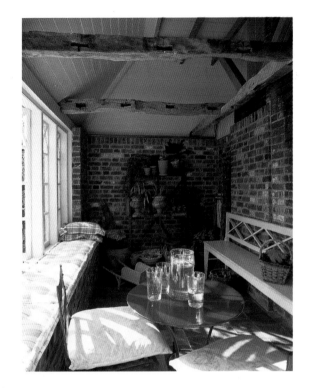

RIGHT: Brian Godbold's garden room was an extension to a 15th-century village row house. It was added in the 19th century as a Victorian laundry shed. On a modern metal table are English hand-blown lemonade glasses from 1875. The plantstand/bench was custom-made by local craftsmen. The plant stand against the brick wall came from antique dealers Richard and Amanda Goodbrey and the metal urns and wheelbarrow from their daughter Sophie Goodbrey who specializes in garden antiques.

Round, sometimes metal-framed and glass topped tables are used, surrounded by folding metal Parc Monceau chairs, or by the fancy, cast-iron chairs with fern or scroll designs so fashionable in the Victorian period. Bentwood chairs with hoop backs, popular from the mid-19th century, or rattan and plain or painted bamboo chairs, all late Victorian favorites, now combine with variations on today's mass-produced plastic chairs. Wicker armchairs from the 1920s to the 1940s are still used, alongside sofas with wide arm rests to hold drinks, with cushions of flowered chintz, canvas, or striped material.

French windows often open onto the garden and, in some cases, have curtains that can be closed for privacy (see page 176). Floors are of stone, tile, or brick, in fact anything that will not be ruined by dripping water and plant debris. At night, candles in hurricane glasses, star-shaped or lantern-like overhead lights, or marquee-style fairy lights, give sparkle to a feast.

A meal in a conservatory, whether large or small, has a special glamour, something akin to the banqueting houses of old – the meal in an unexpected setting. We tend to think of banquets as being huge gatherings, but they were frequently for a small, intimate group of people, held in a separate house that required some kind of excursion. This type of novelty – a journey to Watteau's pleasure isle, *Cythera* – is international, but each country has its own style.

Follies were introduced into the grounds of English country houses in the 18th century, some of them with dining rooms for banqueting. They came in a wide range of whimsical and extravagant styles, from miniature castles and pagodas to the cottage *orné*. A number of them were elaborately plastered inside, such as the Menagerie (see page 115), though marble was a favorite material on floors and walls because it is fairly impervious to the elements. If designed as a Classical Temple of the Winds or a Doric temple, they were open to the outside and unfurnished. Others were formed into grottoes, and here shells were used in abundance as decoration, often interspersed with small pieces of mirror to draw in the light. To complete the effect, a hermit might be paid to stay there as though in a "horrid" cave.

Hagley Hall in Worcestershire was built in 1754–60 by the 1st Lord Lyttleton and commands a splendid view over the hills of the Welsh borders. Here Sanderson Miller, an architect in the Gothick style, designed a ruined castle that was described by Horace Walpole as having "the true rust of the Barons' wars." The most notable ornamental building in the surrounding parkland is, however, a Doric temple designed by James "Athenian" Stuart in 1758–9 and the first archeologically correct recreation of an Ancient Greek temple in Europe, an important step in the developing neo-Classical style.

On a more modest level is the garden house. These can take a variety of forms, from a rusticated twig arbor with benches surrounding a central table to a prefabricated lean-to used to store the croquet set, garden bowls, and hoses. The garden play-cottage that was made for the Royal Princesses in the 1930s had a thatched roof. More recently, Prince Charles built two handsome, neo-Classical, wooden garden houses in his thriving organic gardens at Highgate. At Burton Hall, the home of architect John Roberts – a house with the remains of a Jacobean wing and an 18th-century James Paine facade – a corridor leads to

ABOVE: Part of the conservatory area at Hambledon Hall is set aside for flower-arranging. Baskets and plant containers are stored on and under an old table set against a wall festooned with greenery.

a glass-sided building containing a contemporary swimming pool. At ground level from the pool, sheep and cattle can be seen nibbling the grass right up to the surrounding path. English garden houses are refined in style without forfeiting the bucolic effect. The garden house shown opposite in what was once John Fowler's country retreat has simple plank floors that contrast with the Italianate urns and swags that he insouciantly painted on the walls. Late 18th-century chairs with Gothick-style backs originally surrounded the table. No matter what the style, a garden house makes a perfect retreat for a meal, or just to read a book.

Some country houses have a loggia, in an attempt to catch the sun. These can vary from being a tiny covered space with room for one or two chairs, to a verandah that runs the length of the house and overlooks a specific view. One such verandah, shown above, has been built to overlook a cricket pitch. A loggia may lead onto a stone terrace punctuated by stone urns, Versailles tubs, Lutyens benches, and statuary, and with steps down to a lush green lawn or to a lake.

LEFT: On the verandah of the Munkenbecks' renovated cricket pavilion, an oak table, constructed from the best parts of two damaged tables that had been in the club room from the beginning, has been bolted to the floor.

LEFT BELOW: This private cricket pavilion was built in about 1910 for the family who lived at nearby Westbury House. It has been restored and converted into a second home by architect Alfred Munkenbeck. Though most of the field around it is wild, a circle, 100 yards (91.4 meters) in diameter, has been mown as a landscaping statement.

In summer, the English love tea on the lawn under a shady tree. The English picnic lays less emphasis on going to an organized site where the table and benches are permanently in place, as in America, and more on finding the perfect secluded spot, then laying a picnic cloth right on the grass together with a hamper of sandwiches, lemonade, fruit, a thermos, and, for diehards, a spirit stove for making fresh tea. The 1940s writer Denton Welsh, now a cult figure, took only Ryvita (a type of cracker), chocolate, and an apple as he picnicked his way through the countryside by bike. Elaborate picnics take place on the lawns at Glyndebourne Opera House prior to the performance, a location that can be thought of as a vast roofless room, while superb food, the best a country estate can provide, is offered at a shooting box (a lodge used in the shooting season). Luncheons at the races can include family recipes that date back to the 18th century. Tailgate picnickers at Goodwood bring out deluxe English picnic hampers fitted with champagne glasses and silver cutlery. Children like to escape into a tree house and have secret, delicious meals concocted from bread, butter, and brown sugar, in a place where everything tastes satisfying.

ABOVE: When John Fowler died, designer Nicholas Haslam bought his legendary house in the country. The garden, with its clipped box and a hornbeam allée laid out by Fowler, has matured over the years. This garden house is one of two that face each other across a path. They were designed by Fowler, who also painted grisaille murals inside them.

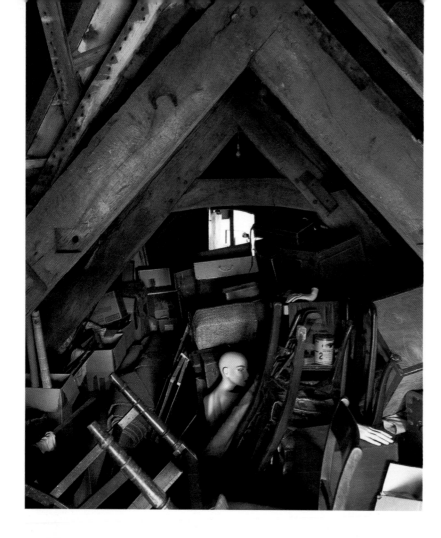

LEFT: The lumber room at Eyam Hall, an attic addict's dream, has had well over 300 years in which to accumulate its cache of mingled trash and treasures.

RIGHT: The attic in a Georgian farmhouse in Norfolk runs the length of the house. In it are stored unused furnishings, bags and suitcases, plus millinery fabrics and hat stands used by the owner in a previous career as a hat designer.

ABOVE: Vintage old luggage – the sort that Ralph Lauren would turn somersaults for – is piled up in an attic corridor in the 1812 Norman Revival castle, Eastnor, in Hereford.

ANOTHER PERIPHERAL ROOM IS THE LOFT AT THE TOP OF THE HOUSE. Sometimes called the attic, lumber room, or box room, it is usually used as storage space. Large trunks – increasingly endangered as useful objects because they are too big for the airline traveler, though too nostalgic to throw away – suitcases, broken chairs, tailors' dummies, baby's cots, magazines, scrapbooks and bundles of letters, lamp stands and shades, rolls of fabric, obsolete gadgets, bags of old buttons, and the toy farm or doll's house awaiting a grandchild, are all part of the remains of everyday life that are packed away in these rooms and often forgotten. Racks of clothes no longer in fashion might include such treasures as top hats in shaped leather cases, uniforms from the Boer War, or a Victorian whalebone crinoline.

Rolls of wallpaper stacked in an attic, still unpacked and pristinely colored after centuries, can be a great source of inspiration for designers; these are the rooms where some of the great documentary wallpaper patterns have been discovered. House historians search for clues among those overlooked but important treasures stored in attics. Sadly, much is lost. It will never be known exactly what was destroyed in the fire at Sledmere in 1911. Though most of the furnishings on the lower floors were removed in time, everything in the attics perished.

Attics are often converted into bedrooms. This must have been the case in the attic shown opposite because a fireplace can be seen at the far end. In the past, maids might have slept in the attics, which were reached by the back stairs. Attics are also now frequently used as studios or sewing rooms, where work can be done in peace at the top of the house. One or two skylights can be created to give the necessary light.

LEFT: The stables at Houghton Hall are constructed of Carr stone from Snettisham, a different stone from the main house which is made of the distinctive creamy gold Aislaby sandstone from Yorkshire. These stables are designed in a simple, robust, early 18th-century style with solid wood pillars, arched windows, herringbone brick floors and beautifully finished wood stalls. William Kent, the genius behind the Palladian beauty of Houghton, had come a long way from his beginnings as a coach and house painter, but must have used his early experience in the aesthetic combination of practicality with great style when designing these stables. The stables surround a handsome central courtyard where a double fountain plashes into a trough.

UNTIL THE 20TH CENTURY, STABLES WERE AN ESSENTIAL OUTER BUILDING that supported the country house. The only means of transport was the horse or shanks's pony. Depending on the size of the house, there might be a carriage house as well as other auxiliary buildings. A number of these still exist, with beautifully preserved carriages displayed alongside polished vintage cars and the latest motorbike.

Stables usually surrounded a central courtyard both in stately homes and in farmhouses, but the scale was different. Farms seldom had carriages, but they did have to accommodate the haywain. Farm stables were for cart horses, and there were always rows of sheds for cattle with hay lofts up above. If solidly built, many of these cowsheds and stables can be converted into dwellings or garages. Farms also had other specialized buildings for animals: kennels, the hen house, the dovecote, beehives, and the pig sty. Though the builder may not have been conscious of it, these shelters were built in a form-follows-function mode that has become part of England's collective memory.

The English room, whether in the town or the country, is less a "look" than a state of mind. It tends to resist conventional categorization and encompasses a medley of diverse influences: old and new, native and exotic, arty and puritan, house and garden. It shows a respect for heritage, a tolerance for "pleasing decay" and "sweet disorder," and a fascination with the unusual and curious. The English admire the best of the new in combination with well-proved heirlooms. To quote decorator Robert Kime: "You never find a blank slate in England." Disciplined craftsmanship, the patina of use, a relaxed attitude to color schemes and pattern-mixing, and a happy blend of the brand-new and hand-me-downs are all traits found in the interiors of homes in England.

ABOVE: The saddle-room in the stables at Calke Abbey, in Derbyshire, reflects the sporting tastes of the Harpur-Crewe family whose lives revolved around animals and hunting for many generations.

USEFUL ADDRESSES & HOUSES TO VISIT

ARCHITECTS, DECORATORS AND DESIGNERS

ALIDAD MAHLOUDJI
The Lighthouse, Gasworks, 2 Michael Road,
London SW6 2AD
Tel: 020 7384 0121; Fax: 020 7384 0122

JUSTIN MEATH BAKER
Architecture and interiors, London
Tel: 020 7491 9900
Website: www.meathbakerdesign.com

SETH STEIN
52 Kelso Place, London W8 5QG
Tel: 020 7376 0005

NINA CAMPBELL
9 Walton Street, London SW3 2JD
Tel: 020 7225 1105

CHARLES BERESFORD CLARK
22 Hans Crescent, London SW1 XOL
Tel: 020 7589 8277

JANE CHURCHILL
116 Garratt Lane, London W18
Tel: 020 8874 6484

COLEFAX & FOWLER
19–23 Grosvenor Hill, London W1K 3QD
Tel: 020 7493 2231; Fax: 020 7499 9910

COWPER-GRIFFITHS ASSOCIATES
Architecture and interiors, Oxford
e-mail: chris.@cowper-griffiths.demon.co.uk

GREENOCK, WESTENHOLZ, GIBBS
76–78 Pimlico Road, London SW1 W8PL
Tel: 020 7823 6667/5

NICHOLAS HASLAM
12 Holbein Place, London SW1
Tel: 020 7730 8623; Fax: 020 7730 6679

DAVID HARE
23 Pembridge Square, London W2 4DR
Tel: 020 7792 2373

INTERIOR DESIGN STUDIO
IMOGEN TAYLOR AND PIERRE SERRURIER
85 Bourne Street, London SW1 W8HF
Tel: 020 7823 4101; Fax: 020 78234062

CATH KIDSTONE
Clarendon Cross, London W11 4AP
Tel: 020 7221 4000

ROBERT KIME
PO Box 454, Marlborough, Wiltshire SN8 3UR
Tel: 01264 731268; Fax: 01264 731203

ROLAND KLEIN
Flat 1, no.16, Bolton Gardens, London SW5 OAJ
Tel: 020 7373 9398

MUNKENBECK AND MARSHALL
Exmouth House, Pine Street, London EC1 ROJH
Tel: 020 7833 11407
e-mail: alfred@mandm.uk.com
(Alfred Munkenbeck)

CHRISTOPHER NEVILE
Manor Farm, Aubourn, Lincoln LN5 9DX
Tel: 01522 788717
e-mail: cnevile@talk21.com

PATTERSON BUXTON
The Nile Street Studios, 8–10 Nile Street,
London N17RF
Tel: 020 7262 5773

JOHN PAWSON
Unit B, 70–78 York Way, London N1 9AG
Tel: 020 7837 2929; Fax: 020 7837 4949
e-mail: e-mail@johnpawson.co.uk

MICHAEL REEVES
91a Pelham Street, London
Tel: 020 7924 6846

WOOLPIT INTERIORS
Stanley Bates, David Cordon and Michael Elles
The Street, Woolpit, Bury St Edmunds,
Suffolk IP30 9SA
Tel: 01359 240895

MELISSA WYNDHAM
6 Sydney Street, London SW3
Tel: 020 7352 2874

ASSOCIATIONS

CIVIC TRUST
17 Carlton Terrace, London SW1Y 5AW
Tel: 020 7930 0914; Fax: 020 7321 0180
Website: www.civictrust.org.uk

ENGLISH HERITAGE
23 Saville Row, London W15 2ET
Tel: 01793 414910
Website: www.english-heritage.org.uk

FOLLY FELLOWSHIP
19 Sandy Walk, Leeds, West Yorks. LS16 9DW
Tel: 0113 261 3673

THE GEORGIAN GROUP
6 Fitzroy Square, London W1P 6DX
Tel: 020 7387 1720; Fax: 020 7387 1721

HISTORIC HOUSES ASSOCIATION
2 Chester Street, London SW1X 7BB
Tel: 020 7259 5688; Fax: 020 7259 5590

THE LANDMARK TRUST
Shottesbrooke, Maidenhead, Berkshire SL6 3SW
Tel: 01628 825952
Website: www.landmarktrust.co.uk

THE NATIONAL TRUST
36 Queen Anne's Gate, London SW1H 9AS
Tel: 020 7222 9251; Fax: 020 7222 5097

THE ROYAL OAK FOUNDATION
(A fund-raising arm of the National Trust,
operating in the USA)
285 West Broadway, New York, NY 10013
Tel: (800) 913-6565 or (212) 229 8925

SAVE BRITAINS' HERITAGE
70 Cowcross Street, London EC1M 6EJ
Tel: 020 7253 3500; Fax: 020 7253 3400
Website: www.savebritainsheritage.org

SOCIETY FOR PROTECTION OF ANCIENT
BUILDINGS
37 Spital Square, London E16 DY
Tel: 020 7377 1644; Fax 020 7247 5296

COURSES

ADDINGHAM Sybil Bruel, 285 Central Park
West, New York, NY 10024
Tel: (212) 362 0701
Web site: www.addinghamtrust.org
Offers a summer course of the study of the
British house and its contents, including
architecture, landscaping, social history,
and furnishings. Main course: July; Shorter
courses: June and September.

PARSON'S SCHOOL OF DESIGN
Office of Special Programs, 66 Fifth Avenue,
New York, NY 10011
Tel: (212) 229-8925
Open enrolment summer design courses are
offered in England, France, Japan, and New
York.

SIR JOHN SOANE'S MUSEUM FOUNDATION
636 Broadway, Suite 720, New York, NY 10012
Tel: (646) 654 0085; Fax: (212) 654.0089
Provides lectures on the work of this English
architect and related subjects and visits to
places of architectural and decorative interest.

SOTHEBY'S INSTITUTE OF ART
1334 York Avenue, New York, NY 10021
Tel: (212) 894 1111
Offers individual lectures and seminar days.

THE VICTORIAN & ALBERT MUSEUM
Cromwell Road, S. Kensington, London SW7 2RI
Tel: 0207 942 2000
Web site: www.vam.ac.uk
Many educational courses are offered.

THE VICTORIAN SOCIETY
219 South 6th Street, Philadelphia, PA 19106
Tel: (215) 627-4252.
Web site: vsasummerschool@aol.com
A design course takes place in June in
Newport, Rhode Island.

THE VICTORIAN SOCIETY SUMMER SCHOOL,
59 Chiswick Green Studios,
1 Evershed Walk, London W4 5BW
Tel: 020 8747 0709
e-mail: summer-school@victorian-society.org.uk
A design course takes place in London in July.

HOUSES OPEN TO THE PUBLIC

BLICKLING HALL (The National Trust)
Blickling, Norfolk NR11 6NF
Tel: 01263 733084; Fax: 01263 1660

BURGHLEY HOUSE
Stamford, Lincolnshire
Tel: 01780 752451; Fax 01780 480125

CALKE ABBEY (The National Trust)
Ticknall, Derby DE73 1LE
Tel: 01332 863822; Fax 01332 865272

CASTLE HOWARD ESTATE LTD
(The Hon. Simon Howard)
York, North Yorkshire YO60 7DA.
Tel: 01653 648333; Fax 01653 648501

CHATSWORTH (Chatsworth House Trust)
Bakewell, Derbyshire DE45 1PP
Tel: 01246 582204; Fax 01246 583536

EASTNOR CASTLE (J. Hervey-Bathurst)
Near Ledbury, Hereford HR8 IRL
Tel: 01531 633160; Fax: 01531 631776

EBBERSTON HALL
(W. de Wend Fenton, Esq.)
Scarborough, Yorkshire

ELTHAM PALACE (English Heritage)
Court Road, London SE9
Tel: 0208 294 2548

ERDDIG (The National Trust)
Nr. Wrexham, Clwyd, Wales LL13 0YT
Tel: 01978 355314

EYAM HALL (R.H.V. Wright)
Eyam, Derbyshire S32 5QW
Tel: 01433 631603; Fax: 01433 631976

FELBRIGG HALL (The National Trust)
Felbrigg, Norfolk NR11 8PR
Tel: 01263 837444; Fax: 01263 837032

GOODWOOD HOUSE
(The Duke of Richmond)
Chichester, West Sussex PO18 0PX
Tel: 01243 755000; Fax: 01243 755005

HELMINGHAM HALL
(Lord and Lady Tollemache)
(Gardens only) Ipswich, Suffolk IP14 6EF
Tel: 01473 890363

HEVER CASTLE (Broadland Properties Ltd)
Hever, Nr Edenbridge, Kent TN8 7NG
Tel: 01732 865224; Fax: 01732 866796

HOLKAM HALL (The Earl of Leicester)
Wells, Norfolk NR23 1AB
Tel: 01328 710227; Fax: 01328 711707

HOUGHTON HALL
(The Marquess of Cholmondeley)
Kings Lynn, Norfolk PE31 6UE
Tel: 01485 528569

IGHTHAM MOTE (The National Trust)
Ivy Hatch, Moto Road, Kent TN15 0NT
Tel: 01732 810378; Fax: 01732 811029

KEDLESTON HALL (The National Trust)
Kedleston, Derby DE22 5JH
Tel: 01332 842191; Fax: 01322 841972

KNOLE (The National Trust)
Sevenoaks, Kent TN15 0RP
Tel: 01732 450608; Fax: 01732 465528

LEIGHTON HOUSE MUSEUM
(administered by The Royal Borough of
Kensington and Chelsea Libraries and Arts Service)
12 Holland Park Road, London W14 8LZ
Tel: 020 7602 3316

SISSINGHURST CASTLE GARDEN
(The National Trust) Sissinghurst, Kent
Tel: 01580 712850

SLEDMERE HOUSE (Sir Tatton Sykes, Bart)
Sledmere, Driffield, Yorks YO25 OXG
Tel: 01377 236637

SIR JOHN SOANE'S MUSEUM
13 Lincoln's Inn Fields, London WC2A 3BP
Tel: 020 7405 2107; Fax: 020 7831 3957
Website: www.soane.org

SPENCER HOUSE
27 St James's Place, London SW1A 1NR
Tel: 020 7499 8620

SUDBURY HALL (The National Trust)
Sudbury, Ashbourne, Derby DE6 5HT
Tel: 01283 585305

SYON HOUSE (The Duke of Northumberland)
Brentford, Middlesex TW8 8JF
Tel: 020 8560 0883; Fax: 020 8568 0936

TIXALL GATEHOUSE (Landmark Trust)
Tixall, Near Stafford, Staffordshire
(1580 gatehouse to be seen from outside only,
or contact The Landmark Trust to rent)

WILTON HOUSE (The Earl of Pembroke)
Salisbury, Wiltshire SP2 OBJ
Tel: 01722 743115; Fax: 01722 744447

INDEX

BIBLIOGRAPHY

Barker, C. M., *Flower Faries of the Seasons*, Blackie & Son, London, 1981

Beeton, Isabella, *Mrs. Beeton's Book of Household Management*, Ward, Lock & Co. Ltd., London, 1909

Bradley-Hole, Christopher, *The Minimalist Garden*, Mitchell Beazley, London, 1999

Calloway, Stephen and Jones, Stephen, *Style Traditions: Recreating Period Interiors*, Rizzoli International, New York, 1990

Calloway, Stephen, *Twentieth Century Decoration*, Weidenfeld and Nicholson, London, 1988

Carter, George, *Living with Plants*. Mitchell Beazley, London, 1998

Colvin, Howard, *Calke Abbey, Derbyshire: A Hidden House Revealed*, Antler Books, London, 1985

Cornforth, John, *English Interiors 1790-1848: The Quest for Comfort*, Barrie & Jenkins, London, 1978

Cornforth, John, *The Inspiration of the Past; Country House Taste in the Twentieth Century*, Viking/Country Life, Harmondsworth, 1985

Csaky, Adrian, and Collins, Ian, *Birds of Creation*, Guy Taplin, Csaky Art, Sonning-on-Thames, 1998

de Pougy, Liane, *My Blue Notebooks*, Harper & Row, New York, 1979

Dent, John, *The Quest for Nonsuch*, London Borough of Sutton Libraries and Arts Services, 1981

Douglas, Murray and Irvine, Chippy, *Brunschwig & Fils Style*, Little Brown & Company, Boston, 1995

Ellis, Estelle and Seebohm, Caroline, *At Home with Books: How Book Lovers Live and Care for their Libraries*, Random House, New York, 1995

Fletcher, Banister, and Banister F., *A History of Architecture*, B.T. Batsford, London

Fowler, John and Cornforth, John, *English Decorating in the 18th Century*, Barrie & Jenkins, London, 1974

Glancy, Jonathan, *Modern*, Mitchell Beazley, London, 2000

Green, Candida Lycett, *Country Life: 100 Favourite Houses*, McMillan, London, 1999

Green, Candida Lycett, *English Cottages*, Weidenfeld and Nicholson, London, 1982

Grun, Bernard, *The Timetables of History*, Simon & Schuster, New York, 1982

Hadfield, Miles, *Gardening in Britain*, Hutchinson, London, 1960

Harris, Cyril M., *Dictionary of Architecture and Construction*, McGraw-Hill, New York, 1975

Harris, John, *No Voice from the Hall: Early Memories of a Country House Snooper*, John Murray, London, 1998

Holloway, Edward Stratton, *The Practical Book of Learning Decoration and Furniture*, J.B. Lippin cott Company, Philadelphia & London, 1926

Hudson's Historic Houses and Gardens including Historic Sites of Interest, Hudson's, 1999

Hunt, John Dixon, and Willis, Peter, *The Genius of the Place: The English Landscape Garden 1620-1820*, Harper & Row, New York, 1975

Jackson-Stops, Gervase, *The English Country House: A Grand Tour*, Little, Brown & Company, Boston, Toronto, 1985

Jackson-Stops, Gervase, *The Treasure Houses of Britain: Five Hundred Years of Private Patronage and Art Collecting*, National Gallery of Art, Yale University Press, New Haven and London, 1885

Jones, Chester, (book of Roger Banks-Pye at Colefax *Inspirational Interiors*

Lancaster, Osbert, *Here of All Places*, Houghton Mifflin Co, Boston, 1958

Lander, Hugh and Rauter, Peter, *English Cottage Interiors*, Weidenfeld and Nicholson, London, 1989

Lees-Milne, Alvide, (ed.) *The Englishman's Room*, Salem House, Topsfield MA, 1986

Lees-Milne, Alvide, (ed.) *The Englishwoman's House*, Salem House, Salem NH, 1984

Mandler, Peter, *The Fall and Rise of the Stately Home*, Yale University Press, New Haven & London, 1997

Montgomery-Massingberd, Hugh, *Great Houses of England and Wales*, Rizzoli International, New York, 1994, Nicholson, London

Osborne, Harold, (ed.) *The Oxford Companion to the Decorative Arts*, Oxford University Press, Oxford, London, 1975

Panati, Charles, *The Browser's Book of Beginnings*, Houghton Mifflin Company, Boston, 1984

Parissien, Steven, *Paladian Style*, Phaidon Press Ltd., London, 1994

Pevsner, Nickolaus, *An Outline of European Architecture*, Penguin Books, Baltimore, 1960

Pevsner, Nikolaus, *The Buildings of England*, Penguin Books, Harmondsworth, 1951

Pick, Michael, *The English Room*, Weidenfeld and Nicholson, London, 1985

Praz, Mario, *An Illustrated History of Interior Decoration from Pompei to Art Nouveau*, Thames and Hudson, London, 1964

Saul, Roger, *Mulberry At Home*, Ebury Press, London, 1999

Scott-James, Anne and Lancaster, Osbert, *The Pleasure Garden: An Illustrated History of British Gardening*, Gambit, Ipswich, 1977

Seebohm, Caroline, *English Country: Living in England's Private Houses*, Clarkson Potter, New York 1987

Strong, Roy; Binney, Marcus; Harris John, *A Celebration of Gardens*, Harper Collins, London, 1991

Strong, Roy; Binney, Marcus; Harris John, *The Destruction of The Country House 1875-1975*, Thames and Hudson, London, 1974

Strong, Roy; Binney, Marcus; Harris John, *The Roy Strong Diaries 1967–1987*, Weidenfeld & Nicholson, London, 1997

Sykes, Christopher Simon, *The Visitors' Book*, Triton Press, Hull, 1978

The National Trust Handbook for Members and Visitors, National Trust, Bromley, Kent, published annually

Thornton, Peter, and Dorey, Helen, *Sir John Soane: The Architect as Collector*, Harry N. Abrams, New York, 1992

Thornton, Peter, *Authentic Décor: 1620-1920*, Weidenfeld and Nicholson, London

Thornton, Peter, F*orm & Decoration: Innovation in the Decorative Arts 1470–1870*, Harry N. Abrams, New York, 1998

Tyack, Geoffrey, and Brindle, Steven, *Blue Guide: Country Houses of England*, A & C Black, London, W.W. Norton, New York, 1994

Valentine, Deborah, (ed.) *Historic Houses Castles & Gardens in Great Britain and Ireland*, Reed Information Services, East Grinstead, 1996

Yarwood, Doreen, *The English Home*, B.T. Batsford Ltd, London, 1979

PERIODICALS

Bolton, Lavinia, "Something in Disguise", *House & Garden*, Aug. 1998

Buchan, Ursula, "Natural Preserve of a Lady", *Country Life*, Oct. 12 2000

Cecil, Mirabel, "Best of Fens", *The World of Interiors*, Dec. 1994

Cecil, Mirabel, "Less than Perfect", *The World of Interiors*, Mar. 1998

Cox, Anna Somers, "Eastnor Castle", *The World of Interiors*, Mar. 1998

Digby, Will Wingfield, "Bowled over by Village Cricket", *Country Life*, Aug. 31 2000

Ducas, June, "An English Place that holds an Art Deco Dream", *The New York Times*, Thursday, July 22 1999

Garrat, Pat, "Colefax's Bossy Client", *The World of Interiors*, Mar. '97

Garrat, Pat, "Not so Quick Silver", *The World of Interiors*, Jan. 1996

Hall, Michael, "Sticking to the Plot", *Country Life*, Sept. 26 1996

Musson, Jeremy, "Eltham Palace: London", *Country Life*, June 17 1999

Musson, Jeremy, "The Manor House at Clifton Hampden, Oxfordshire: The home of Mr. Christopher Gibbs", *Country Life*, Oct. 26 2000

Pearman, Hugh, "Kingdom of the Shore", *The World of Interiors*, Mar. '97

Reginato, James, "Kime Times", *The World of Interiors*, Sept. 1999

Robinson, John Martin, "Home House", *Country Life*, December 21 2000

Saachi, Doris Lockhart. "Fresh Eyre", *The World of Interiors*, December 1997

Sackville-West, Robert, "Knole", *The National Trust*, 1998